THE STO.AND

This book tells the fascinating story of sport in England, from its earliest beginnings in social play and pastimes, via its adoption as an alternative to the routine of urban life, to its consumption as the product of a global industry.

Along the way, key themes and issues in the history of sport are examined, including:

- The role of social structures – the influence of society on sport, and sport on society

- The emergence of sport 'welfarism' and 'sport for all'

- The growth of the popular press, and the television revolution

- Globalisation and the sports industry

- Twenty-first century sport – the present and future of sport and leisure.

The Story of Sport in England is an accessible and comprehensive history for A-level students and undergraduates, and an ideal introduction for anyone with an interest in sport history.

Neil Wigglesworth is Honorary Research Fellow in the Department of History at Lancaster University, UK.

STUDENT SPORT STUDIES
Series Editors: Frank Galligan and J.A. Mangan

This is a new series specifically for school, college and university students, written clearly and concisely by expert teachers. The series covers a range of relevant topics for those studying physical education, sports studies, leisure and recreation studies and related courses. Each volume is purposefully prepared for students facing specific course syllabuses and examinations and is sharply focused and written in plain English. The series is in response to repeated requests from students and teachers for accessible books concentrating on courses and examinations.

Frank Galligan
J.A. Mangan

The Olympic Games Explained
A student guide to the evolution of the modern Olympic Games
Vassil Girginov and Jim Parry

Acquiring Skill in Sport
An introduction
John Honeybourne

In Pursuit of Excellence
Michael Hill

THE STORY OF SPORT
IN ENGLAND

NEIL WIGGLESWORTH

Routledge
Taylor & Francis Group

LONDON AND NEW YORK

First published 2007
by Routledge
2 Park Square, Milton Park, Abingdon, Oxon OX14 4RN

Simultaneously published in the USA and Canada
by Routledge
270 Madison Ave, New York, NY 10016

Routledge is an imprint of the Taylor & Francis Group, an informa business

© 2007 Neil Wigglesworth

Typeset in Mixage by
HWA Text and Data Management, Tunbridge Wells

Printed and bound in Great Britain by
MPG Books Ltd, Bodmin

British Library Cataloguing in Publication Data
A catalogue record for this book is available from the British Library

Library of Congress Cataloging-in-Publication Data
Wigglesworth, Neil
The Story of Sport in England / Neil Wigglesworth.
     p. cm. (Student sport studies)
Includes bibliographical references and index.
1. Sports–England–History. 2. Sports–Social aspects–England–History. I Title. II. Series.
GV605.W545 2007
796.334 0942–dc22   2004030462

ISBN10: 0-415-35381-6 (hbk)   ISBN13: 978-0-415-35381-6 (hbk)
ISBN10: 0-415-37264-X (pbk)   ISBN13: 978-0-415-37264-0 (pbk)
ISBN10: 0-203-34742-0 (ebk)   ISBN13: 978-0-203-34742-3 (ebk)

FOR NADYA AND BORIS
MY TWO CHAMPIONS

CONTENTS

ILLUSTRATIONS

Figures

Tables

FOREWORD

History is possibly the most important subject that we can study since it provides us with vital knowledge of past events which may help to solve present and future problems. There are many types of history, the most important of which, I think, is that which deals with people and their everyday lives, in other words social history. Arguably, the most useful and interesting aspect of social history concerns sport since what people choose to do in their leisure time is a wonderful indicator of trends in society at large. When we study sports history we are looking at a microcosm of our national life and the story of sport in England reflects the developments in our society in a way that no other aspect of social history does.

In this book I have tried to let the players tell their own sporting stories by using material from club minute books, a list of which can be found at the end. Using this list it will be possible for you to do some of your own research into what is called 'original source material'; better still, go to your local reference library or records office and dig up some similar documents for yourself. Formal, catalogued material is only available for the last couple of centuries or so and before that I have had to rely on social commentaries, eye-witness accounts and newspaper reports. It has been difficult to provide detailed references for all quotations and sources, however where possible, references are listed.

Between William FitzStephen commenting on boys playing football in the twelfth century and the mega, global event which will be the London Olympics of 2012 lie over eight centuries of recorded history concerning sport. This is our sporting heritage which has provided us with the defining quality of our national character. It is, alongside the English language itself, perhaps the most important contribution made by the people of this country to the world. We only need to think of 'fair play', 'front foot', 'benefit of the doubt', 'level playing field' and many, many other similar phrases to realise how our sporting heritage has moulded the national character and been exported around the world. To enquire into the ways in which our sporting heritage has grown and is still developing is, I believe, not only important in itself but a significant way of monitoring our growth as a nation.

Finally, I'd like to make the point that sport is for playing not watching. As you will read in chapter ten, the younger generation is in danger of becoming obese and unfit through too much sitting and watching. During the next few years as 2012 approaches, you will have many sporting opportunities offered to you by schools and clubs - take them! Your life will be immeasurably improved by involvement in any one of dozens of activities. Not only will you get physically fit with all the health benefits that this will bring but you will experience the exhilaration felt by all the people in this book across the centuries when they played their favourite sports. In that way you will be the inheritors of their tradition and be writing the latest chapter in the great story of English sport.

chapter one

PREVIEW – WHAT THIS BOOK IS ABOUT

NO sport can be insulated from the wider society in which it is played.
(Dunning and Sheard 1979, p. 7)

It is only relatively recently that the ways in which people enjoyed themselves have been seen as an important part of social history. As long ago as the sixteenth century, there were books of instruction on field sports like hunting with dogs and hawks and these followed earlier books about the ways that 'knights at arms' should behave.

It is important to realise that in those days, there were sports for gentlemen and other sports for those lower down the social scale. Some of these activities, such as football and bowling, were banned as 'unlawful' because they were associated with hooligan-like behaviour in the streets. It was also felt that such activities distracted youngsters from practising archery, a skill that could be used to defend the country from attack. England had been at war with either France or Spain for centuries and there was ongoing concern that this might happen again.

Partition and gentrification

Things changed quite a lot during the eighteenth century, due largely to an increase in commercial activity, particularly in London. More people than ever before had money to spend and they increasingly did so on recreational activities such as renting river boats, visiting pleasure gardens and amusement parks, and gambling on sporting contests.

Gradually, this led to a mixing of the classes so that gentlemen became involved with those of 'lower stations' for the first time.

Many of the old upper and new middle classes did not approve of this and established clubs of their own that excluded those considered to be socially inferior.

The division between amateur and professional sport was based on social class and not simply whether or not players were paid for playing.

Increased commercialism also saw a growth in professional sports, the most popular of which were:

■ cricket

■ horse racing

■ boxing

■ running

■ rowing.

Many early professionals were employed by gentlemen who often won or lost thousands on the performances of their 'champions'. Eventually, some of these competitors became independent of their employers and began to earn their own money from prize-funds and from their own gambling.

The growth of 'amateurism'

Members of the growing and increasingly influential middle class – many of whom had been to public school – didn't like this behaviour and reacted by excluding even more people from their own amateur clubs. The word 'amateur' comes from the Latin word 'amare', which means 'to love'.

From the middle of the nineteenth century onwards, amateur and professional sport developed separately with the former being dominant in suburban and countryside areas, whilst professionalism thrived in the towns. This was particularly so in the north of England, where the greater proportion of working people would either take part in sport or pay to watch it.

One century later, after World War II, the two sides of sport moved closer together as amateur clubs became gradually less exclusive and professional sport became more specialised and difficult to enter.

In order to be successful in international competition it became necessary for the amateurs to be more 'professional' in their preparation and both clubs and governing bodies adopted a much more 'open door' policy for new members. Examples of such governing bodies were:

- Amateur Athletic Association
- Amateur Rowing Association
- Amateur Swimming Association
- Lawn Tennis Association.

This development is one example of the way in which society was becoming far more tolerant during the last half of the twentieth century, due primarily to the growth of the welfare state, the introduction of comprehensive education, the consumer revolution, easier communication and travel – and, of course, television.

If we look back at eight centuries of sporting history, we could say that the 'class culture' of the sixteenth century has been largely replaced by the 'cash culture' of the twenty-first century. It is also quite clear that sport affects society and is in turn affected by it.

If we look at the five factors that determined the development of sport, we can see examples of this:

- social factors: e.g. the class-based split between gentlemen amateurs and (largely) working-class professionals
- cultural factors: e.g. the change over centuries from 'class' to 'cash' culture
- political factors: e.g. the outlawing of some sports in order to reduce hooliganism and encourage archery
- economic factors: e.g. the prosperity of eighteenth-century London which kick-started the commercial revolution in sport
- geographical factors: e.g. the difference between 'town' and 'country' and 'north' and 'south' in terms of sports development.

It is also evident that sport is a complicated subject and different sports illustrate different aspects of social development. Cricket, for example, was a simple country sport played with a stick and ball in a field and is now a sophisticated game played in large stadia all over the world.

Sports as a 'convenience'

Wealthy gentlemen and aristocrats found that cricket was an ideal vehicle for gambling and they paid teams of good players to play each other so that they could bet on the result. Cheating was common because everyone wanted to win the huge amounts of money involved. Other examples of sport used in this way by the nobility included:

- horse racing and George III
- running and the Duke of Cumberland
- rowing and the Duke of Richmond
- boxing and the Earl of Derby
- greyhound racing and the Lord Orford.

It was not long before these activities began to attract huge crowds and sports promotion became one of the big businesses of the eighteenth century. Cricket grounds and racecourses were built with grandstands and enclosures where the wealthier customers paid in order to be separated from the ordinary spectators.

Those gentlemen who did participate in sport separated themselves from the lower classes by establishing exclusive clubs and co-operated to form governing bodies for their sports. They then drew up regulations that made it impossible for poorer people to take part. Early examples of these were:

- The Jockey Club – 1750
- The Royal and Ancient Golf Club – 1754
- The Marylebone Cricket Club – 1787
- The Leander Club (rowing) – 1818.

Sport and the public house

Many sports continued to use public houses or taverns as centres for activity as they had for centuries and so, for instance, fox hunters and cross-country horse racers always used taverns as meeting places. Other examples are:

- boxing – the Adam and Eve Tavern, Chelsea
- cock fighting – the White Lion in Brighton

- cricket – the White Head in Leicester
- rowing – the Red Barn in Battersea

These taverns often had ex-sportsmen as landlords, who, when they retired, continued this tradition by selling the premises to other sportsmen. One good example of this was Harry Clasper, the rowing hero, who owned the Queen's Head in Gateshead. He was only one of many sporting personalities who became well known all over the country during the nineteenth century due to appearances in competitions which were prominently reported in newspapers and sporting magazines.

The popularity of these sporting champions, particularly in the north of England, made sports governing bodies even more determined to exclude professionals and if possible get rid of professional sport altogether. The new middle-class 'public school men' who ran these bodies began to call professional sportsmen 'unmanly, unchristian and unpatriotic' and drew up new rules to further exclude them from any competition that was organised under their auspices.

The public house has long provided a sporting outlet for ordinary people. As the open space in towns was lost to industrial development, it was often the public house that afforded what little recreational space could be found – in the form of a skittle alley or a bowling green.

'Unholy' alliances

One result of the social exclusions referred to above was the formation of rival organisations in the north of England prepared to accept these 'professionals'. New sports like rugby league were established to cater for this new situation. These new organisations included:

- The Northern Rugby Union
- Northern Cross Country Association
- Northern Counties Athletic Association.

Many northern sports formed leagues in order to facilitate regular competition and promotion and relegation. This stimulated even greater interest for the spectators who would watch in ever-greater numbers.

These and other promotional changes were so successful in football that people in the south of England began to call it 'a passion, not a recreation'.

5

These words, 'passion' and 'recreation', reflect the two different attitudes to sport taken by the working and middle classes. Working people had to cram as much enjoyment as possible into the little recreation time they had whilst the middle classes had far more leisure time. Another important factor was the space available to the two classes. Working people lived in (typically) tiny terraced houses whilst their betters lived in suburban semi-detached homes with gardens.

These differing attitudes to sport led to the development of two different sporting cultures. One was centred largely in the industrial areas of the north and midlands whilst the other was to be found in the Home Counties around London. There were some areas where working-class and middle-class sport co-existed and we will visit some of these in due course.

This separation led middle-class people to abandon sports such as football and to take up sports that they could play either in small private local clubs or in their own back gardens. These exclusive middle-class sports included such activities as:

- lawn tennis
- croquet
- archery.

During the Victorian and Edwardian eras, this separation grew as working people gained more free time and had a little more money to spend.

Evidence of this can be seen in the record membership levels of amateur clubs following World War I, which coincided with record crowds attending professional games of rugby league and association football.

Middle-class sport grew with the spread of suburbia and sports clubs grew up in these areas. In order of popularity they were:

- golf
- rugby
- tennis
- cricket
- rowing.

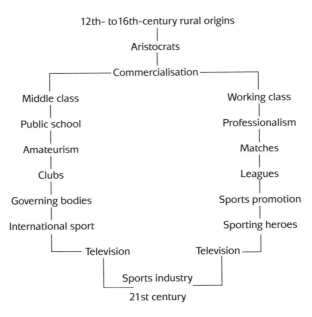

```
                12th- to16th-century rural origins
                              |
                         Aristocrats
                              |
              ┌───────── Commercialisation ──────────┐
              |                                       |
        Middle class                           Working class
              |                                       |
        Public school                         Professionalism
              |                                       |
        Amateurism                               Matches
              |                                       |
           Clubs                                  Leagues
              |                                       |
      Governing bodies                        Sports promotion
              |                                       |
    International sport                        Sporting heroes
              └─── Television          Television ───┘
                        |              |
                    └── Sports industry ──┘
                        21st century
```

FIGURE 1.1   Diagrammatic representation of sporting development

Reconciling the irreconcilable

We have already noted that amateur and professional sports have come together over the last half century, due largely to the pressures and national prestige surrounding international competition. Because of this governments have become increasingly involved in the administration of sport. This was evident in the creation of the Sports Development Council (1965), which was responsible for implementing a 'Sport for All' policy.

However, the single most important factor has undoubtedly been television; particularly since satellite technology has afforded live coverage of sporting events from around the world. We could say that sport is no longer in the hands of the players or the spectators – or even governments – but of global television corporations.

In this review of English sport from the twelfth to the twenty-first century we have seen a variety of developments and we will revisit them in more detail later in this book.

Suggested further reading

Dunning, E. and Sheard, K., *Barbarians, Gentlemen and Players* (Robertson, 1979)

Ford, J., *This Sporting Land* (New English Library, 1977)

Plumb, J., *The Growth of Leisure 1630–1830* (Oxford University Press, 1972)

chapter two

THE ORIGINS OF SPORT

Unlawful games such as boleng is comynly used at all divers tymes so
that the maytenance of Archery is cleane left unexiecysed.
(Southampton Court Records, 1569)

It has always been common for gentlemen to use their recreations as
badges of social and physical superiority over the lower orders.
(Marcia Vale, in 'Gentlemen's Recreations' 1580–1630, p. 4)

Joseph Strutt, in *The Sports and Pastimes of the People of England* (1801),
described many English sports and most of them were ancient even then. We
know this because FitzStephen also describes them in his twelfth-century *History
of London* where he mentions the sports enjoyed by people on religious holidays,
including, in the summer:

- jumping
- dancing
- wrestling
- throwing
- fighting with shields

and in the winters:

- sliding
- sledging

- curling
- hockey.

These activities took place all around the country but we have particular evidence of them being enjoyed in the more prosperous towns of London, Oxford, York, Lincoln and Norwich and in smaller places that had regular weekly markets.

The most popular sport was football and important games were often held on Shrove Tuesday, when all the able-bodied men (and sometimes women) of one village played those of another using all the country in between as the pitch.

Other sports regularly played on Sundays were wrestling, boxing and bowling all of which presented opportunities for gambling and drinking since the taverns were always open for business.

It is not surprising that such enthusiastic play on Sundays resulted in people taking Mondays off work (popularly known as 'Saint Monday') and it was largely because of this that governments began to legislate against gambling, drinking and the games themselves. In fact the best way of discovering which games were the most popular is to look at court records to find how many people were prosecuted for playing them. Such research tends to show that apart from football, the sports played most often and which caused most disruption were:

- bowls
- tennis
- hockey
- skittles.

Unruly recreations

In 1477, the disturbances from these sports became so bad that Edward IV levied heavy fines for playing them. Court records show that eleven men were fined a week's wages each for playing bowls at Ampthill in Bedfordshire in 1502 and some boys had to pay twelve pence each for playing tennis. In addition to their fines, they were served with the mediaeval equivalent of a Community Service Order and told to practise for several hours at the 'butts' (the local archery range).

In those days many games had no rules and it was not unusual for players in football, for instance, to be badly hurt or even killed; in which event, 'death by football' would be written in the coroner's record book.

10

Bowls and skittles were also sometimes fatal since they used heavy wooden balls which were lethal in the hands of angry and often drunken players. Some regulation was introduced when bowling greens and skittle alleys were built in or near taverns and by the eighteenth century they had been brought largely under control.

By the end of the fifteenth century tennis equipment had improved to meet the demands of the wealthier players who had their own courts and this led to better standards of play, closer competition and, in turn, to new rules.

Poorer people played a game called 'field tennis' that did not require the elaborate enclosed wooden courts of 'real' or 'royal' tennis.

Activities such as fishing and fowling were restricted to landowners and anyone else found doing either was dealt with as a poacher. It is interesting to note that a book entitled *Treatise on Fyssynge with an Angle* (1496) maintained that fishing was a therapeutic activity 'good for the body and the soul'. This was also said about football by Richard Mulcaster in his book, *The Schoolmaster*, published in 1561.

This was then a most unusual attitude and did not become fashionable until the nineteenth century when sport became an important social, political and educational tool of government. It seems, however, that Elizabeth I was impressed by the therapeutic quality of sport, as in 1573 she referred to Ralphe Bowes as 'the master of our game, pastymes and sportes' when she appointed him the first ever Minister of Sport.

Although there was little mixing of the classes in sport, this did sometimes happen at cock fights or bull/bear baiting contests. However, the gentry often found vantage points that separated them from the rest. In cockpits there were raised areas at the rear where a better view could be had without mingling with the 'common people'.

Even spectating could be dangerous. In March 1526 at the Paris Gardens bear pit in Southwark, London, a brown bear known as 'The Poet' broke free from his chains and killed a spectator by biting his head off.

Gentlemanly pursuits

Apart from various forms of hunting, other popular 'gentry' pursuits included:

- archery
- fencing

- dancing
- golf
- swimming
- tennis
- bowling.

Tennis and bowls were popular with all classes but were played in very different surroundings. Bowling for the common man began with throwing stones at a stake in the ground, which led to damage when players disagreed. The popularity of the game kept people from work, causing it to be banned by Edward II in 1349.

Meanwhile, gentlemen played the game on finely cropped grass and the first evidence of this is found in Southampton when in 1299 a 'Master of the Green' was elected at God's House hospital. The Guild of Grocers opened the first public bowling green in London in 1433.

For centuries this 'common game' caused social disruptions and court records show many prosecutions like the one against nineteen players in May 1577 (again in Southampton) for injury to people and property in one of the town's main streets.

Although James I began to allow the playing of some previously unlawful sports on Sundays, the one exception to this was *boleng*. The reason given by James for this amnesty was that to ban them caused religious intolerance among the common people and that playing them 'made their bodies more able for warr'.

Similarly, tennis, which evolved in its genteel form from ball games played in monasteries, derived its common form as a result of people handling any light object over obstructions such as walls, hedges or ditches.

Tennis was very popular with ordinary people and was recorded as unlawful in warrants and proclamations issued by the monarch. It did, however, become popular with the wealthier classes, who by 1500 had constructed at least ten very expensive tennis 'courts' in the centre of London – the first of which was in Culver Alley in 1459.

Both bowling and tennis eventually became widely accessible to ordinary people with the development of public parks and the provision of workplace recreational facilities in the second half of the nineteenth and the early twentieth century.

The butts

Ordinary men were required to practise archery for the defence of the realm and saw it largely as a chore. The longbow was the weapon of the lowly foot soldier but those who could afford a horse preferred the rather superior role of the cavalryman. The growth of military mercenaries during the fifteenth century meant that there was less need for skilled bowmen and this together with alternatives such as football and bowls, led to the decline of archery amongst ordinary people.

Archery practice was required by law until the end of the sixteenth century, by which time the bow had become obsolete as a weapon of war and archery grounds ('butts') were becoming derelict. The butts in Alport Lane, Manchester (now part of Deansgate), was repaired in 1576 but two years later it was again derelict and unused.

Although longbows and crossbows had long been used by gentlemen for hunting they had been replaced by the musket by the middle of the sixteenth century and those interested in archery as a recreation turned to target archery using straw targets.

The first mention of a competition, at Scorton in Yorkshire on May 14th, 1673, described the event as 'ancient', so it may be that the original *Scorton Arrow* event was then at least a century old. So, just as the ordinary man was released from the chore of archery, the gentry took it up as a recreation!

Shooting

From the mid-sixteenth century onwards, the gentry used muskets for hunting. Shooting with a gun became uniquely their sport, representing as it did, their social and financial superiority over the ordinary man. During the eighteenth century, the mass production of muskets to supply the new militia (established to counter civil unrest) brought prices down and 'rough' shooting became popular with a wider cross section of society. This resulted in the killing of vast numbers of wildlife with the result that the sport was made more exclusive by means of:

- expensively conserving game
- introducing shooting licences
- establishing a closed season.

All of the above had the effect of reducing the number of people who could afford to participate. This 'exclusivity' is maintained today because of:

- ecological pressures on wildlife
- private ownership of shooting land
- high costs of fees and equipment.

Hunting

Hunting has also retained its privileges over the centuries. It was inevitably restricted to horse owners and initially pursued only by the nobility but did later spread to the more prosperous yeoman farmers.

Hunting of all kinds was severely curtailed following the Norman Conquest, when the penalty for illegal possession of game was the loss of a limb. (The origin of the expression 'costing an arm and a leg'.)

The Charter of the Forests (1217) softened these penalties and placed limits on the extent of the royal hunting grounds. However, following the Peasants' Revolt of 1389, Richard II decreed that the pursuit of game was lawful only for those qualified by ownership of land.

Hunting, fishing and shooting were practised 'for fun' by the upper echelons of society and 'for survival' by those less fortunate. It was not uncommon for the peasantry to engage in the same activities as their 'betters' … but for different reasons and often illegally.

Following the seventeenth-century invasion of hunting by the growing middle class Charles II introduced a gentleman's 'game privilege' based on high land ownership (quantity of land owned), so that despite the social progress of the intervening centuries hunting is still a sport for the relatively prosperous.

The turf

Horse racing grew naturally from the competition to be the first to the kill in hunting. Racing always had strong royal support and had become a fashionable pastime of the nobility by the twelfth century.

However, it was not until 1540 that the first racecourse (The Rhoodee) was established at Chester. James I established racing at Newmarket, Doncaster, York and London and Charles II made Newmarket the sport's headquarters, riding his own horse to victory there in 1671.

By 1750 the popularity of the sport was such that the aristocrats of Newmarket formed the Jockey Club and protected their privileged access to Newmarket

Heath by excluding all non-members. Like other sports, racing had its attendant cheating and gambling, which necessitated the introduction of rules to control these activities. One of the first sets of rules was the *Rules of Racing*, written by Richard Legh in 1680 when he built his racecourse at Newton Heath in Lancashire (now Haydock Park).

For a time, the 'fixing' of races gained the sport a bad reputation and many aristocrats abandoned the sport altogether, following the Duke of Dorset's advice to take up cricket, which, he said, 'made much better use of the turf'.

The early days of cricket

Cricket began like other stick and ball games:

- stob ball
- stow ball
- stump ball
- trap ball
- bandy wicket.

All of the above were played regularly in the countryside using whatever implements came to hand.

Cricket was probably derived from a combination of these games with the 'wicket' being added as a target for the bowler. The bat may well have been a shepherd's crook and the ball made of wool.

The temporary decline of horse racing encouraged gentlemen to take up cricket, with many sponsoring village clubs such as the one at Hambledon in Hampshire which was regarded at the time as having the best players in the country, e.g. David Harris and 'Lumpy' Stevens. The aristocrats would use their own servants in matches against such clubs and, of course, gamble on the result.

It was not long before the game was taken into London at places like White Conduit Fields and Mary-le-Bone and rules introduced in an attempt to reduce the level of gambling in the sport.

When the gentlemen sent their children to the new public schools, the game of cricket went with them and has since become a national game alongside the ancient sport of football.

'Grandstands' were constructed at racecourses and cricket grounds in order to afford a restricted area where the upper classes could meet with their equals free of the unseemly habits of those of the lower orders. This also provided additional sources of income for racecourse owners and was copied when football grounds were enclosed.

Football persists

Despite the twenty-three edicts banning it, football continued to be the national pastime for the lower orders and it was played – often without rules – at every opportunity. Packs of men and boys caused disruption by playing in the most inconvenient of places, just as the 'companies of lewd and disordered persons who spilled into the streets and broke windows' did in Manchester in 1603.

The gentry attempted to adapt the game for their own use by building 'futebale crofts', which restricted the area of play. They also introduced rules and their children eventually played the game at school – under strict supervision.

By the fifteenth century, the Fraternity of Footballers had been established and in 1421 hired the Brewers' Hall in the City of London to hold their annual dinner.

It seems likely that football challenge matches took place between the craft guilds at several venues and these games would be played on a restricted field some 220 yards (200 metres) long with thirty players on each side.

This 'field football' gradually became the preferred form of the game as more people moved into towns and the old 'cross-country' football declined and eventually disappeared. The disruptive behaviour associated with 'unlawful sports' was not apparently restricted to those played on land and FitzStephen mentions that water-quintain (jousting using boats rather than horses) often degenerated into a general free for all.

Boatmen and the prize ring

The watermen of London who ferried people up and down the Thames were well known for their outrageous behaviour, which included 'wager racing' in the seventeenth century. Here individual 'Oscullers' competed for what were often large 'wagers' or money bets.

In 1715, Thomas Doggett, a well-known actor, left money in his will to be rowed for every year and this race (the winner is awarded a ceremonial coat and badge – and originally a new boat) is thought to be one of the oldest sporting competitions in the world.

Even in this race the contestants often tried to foul each other and all were bombarded with objects thrown at them from bridges as they rowed underneath. Boats were also rented out to the general public and often used by youngsters to cause all kinds of trouble to other river users. This caused the Lord Mayor to prohibit their use on Sundays and even local headmasters banned pupils from rowing to reduce the number of tragic accidents.

One of the early winners of the Doggett Coat and Badge Race, Jack Broughton (1730), used boxing as a form of training and when he retired from the river he became a physical fitness trainer to the gentry. Gentlemen paid him to get them fit and to instruct their footmen in the art of 'pugilism'. This was so that they could be matched against other boxers and provide yet more opportunities for gambling.

Broughton became known as the 'Father of British Boxing' because he introduced a scientific approach to what had previously been simply brawling. He also established certain rules governing what was and what was not permissible in the ring.

Pugilism was only one of several violent sports to be found at that time. Others included:

- Cornish wrestling
- Cumbrian wrestling
- cudgel fighting
- shin kicking.

Injuries were frequent, with broken backs in wrestling, cracked skulls, broken noses and smashed eyes in cudgelling and broken legs in shin kicking. It should be remembered that in those times life expectancy for the ordinary man and woman was around forty years and such dangers were simply part of life.

Gentlemen rarely took part in such activities except to gamble on them but they were taught sword fighting or fencing as social accomplishments. Strangely enough, the person who taught these activities might have also taught them dancing since agility was necessary for both.

Dancing was, however, frowned upon for working-class men and women because it was always associated with bad behaviour or, as James I said in his *Book of Sports* (1617), 'with lewd behaviour, filthie typlinge and drunkeness'.

Generally, however, James defended the rights of ordinary folk to enjoy their recreations – particularly on the Sabbath:

> **... For when shall the common people have leave to exercise, if not upon the Sundayes and holy daies, seeing they must apply their labour and win their living in all working days?**

Golf and hockey

These two ancient games were both essentially the same activity – hitting small objects with a bent stick. All social classes in Scotland had played golf for centuries in the sand dunes, which were regarded as common land open to all.

The records of Alnmouth Golf Club in Northumberland as recently as 1907 also state that, 'the working classes who reside in the village of Alnmouth can play on the course without membership'.

Hockey, like football, was often played by crowds of people and was often prohibited by the authorities. Like other games, it was gradually taken over by the upper classes and eventually found its way into public schools and other such establishments.

Going to the dogs ...

Initially, all classes also used dogs for hunting until the first 'forest laws' introduced by the Normans forbade their use by commoners who used them to catch food.

The gentry, however, used dogs in pursuit of game as a means of racing them and this was so popular that in 1580 the Duke of Norfolk drew up the 'Laws of the Leash'.

This form of dog racing eventually became hare coursing using the greyhound – the fastest dog available – and in a reversal of the normal trend in the evolution of sport, the working class embraced the idea of coursing and turned it into whippet and greyhound racing in specially built stadiums – another rural sport becoming an urban recreation!

Swimming and running

Unlike golf and dog racing, swimming and running maintained a strict separation of classes. Swimming was thought to be a gentlemanly skill with military origins in Greek antiquity and fashion during the seventeenth century persuaded gentlemen

Common form	Sports	Gentrified form
	Common form	**Gentrified form**
Hunting/military	**Archery**	Target
Field	**Bowls**	Bowling green
Field	**Boxing**	Boxing ring
Barnyard	**Cock-fighting**	Cockpit
Field	**Cricket**	Cricket ground
Cross-country	**Dog-racing**	Field
Cross-country	**Football**	Field
Sand dunes	**Golf**	Golf course
Cross-country	**Hockey**	Field
Cross-country	**Horse racing**	Race course
Field	**Tennis**	Tennis court

FIGURE 2.1   The effect of gentrification on sporting development

(not ladies) that swimming in salt water was therapeutic. This notion began with Everard Digby's *Scientific Treatise on Swimming*, published in 1587.

Running was out of the question for gentlemen but footmen and servants were encouraged to do so in order that their masters might gamble on the result.

Common men would run for prizes at rural sports events and at specially staged urban 'games' such as those at Kersal Moor in Manchester where, throughout the sixteenth century, prizes included food, drink or clothing.

This chapter explains that our national sports grew from common roots but developed differently because of social concerns and the need for civil security. Originally the master and 'his man' occupied separate social and cultural worlds but the eventual increase in commercial activity and the growth of a 'middling class' encouraged a mingling of the classes which is now well represented in sport. More of this in the next chapter.

THE ORIGINS OF SPORT

1   Explain the importance of the public house in the development of sport.

2   Explain the difference between 'gentlemanly pursuits' and 'unruly recreations.

3   What were the social and financial reasons for the building of grandstands at sporting venues?

4   Why was the playing of football by ordinary men and boys frowned upon?

5   What was Jack Broughton's contribution to boxing?

6   Gentlemen rarely competed in pugilistic or similar contests but were taught sparring, sword fighting or fencing by professional instructors. Why was this?

Suggested further reading

Holt, R., *Sport and the British* (Oxford University Press, 1989)

Mason, A., *Sport in Britain* (Faber & Faber, 1988)

Walvin, J., *Leisure and Society* (Longman, 1978)

chapter three

THE COMMERCIALISATION OF SPORT

There was a prodigious conflux of nobility and gentry into London.
(D. Defoe, 1726)

Purses of £50 entered at the Cross Keys.
No horse to stand at any house that does not subscribe 1 guinea.
Cocking at The Woolpack as usual.
(Notice for Warwick Races, August 1783)

Public houses and taverns had always been centres of recreation providing for such activities as bowling, skittles, cock-fighting and hunting. Publicans were amongst the first commercial sponsors of sporting activity. Town councils also sponsored horse racing to attract people to their area, much as tourist boards and chambers of commerce do today.

Newton racecourse in Lancashire (now Haydock Park) was established by the Lord of the Manor, Richard Legh, who ensured that all the local innkeepers made an annual donation of twelve pence towards a silver plate 'to be run for with horses'. All the prizes were funded by commercial subscription or donations from local nobility.

Sporting pubs and taverns

Local inns would make handsome profits from selling food and drink to the race-goers and by staging cock-fights (for gambling) after the day's racing. 'Cocking' – as it was known – often resulted in violent disputes and although it was banned throughout the country in 1795, it remains popular in certain areas today, with a prosecution being brought in Kellow, County Durham as recently as 1995.

Inns also provided social facilities for sportsmen. The most famous being 'The Bat and Ball' on Hambledon Down in Hampshire, which, during the eighteenth century, hosted a village cricket team that beat all-comers.

Publicans soon realised that sport had a commercial appeal and in London cricket games attracted very large crowds. This applied particularly to unusual games such as the match in August 1778 featuring one-armed and one-legged ex-servicemen.

A newly opened inn would often stage a contest to publicise itself, such as the match between married and unmarried women sponsored by 'The Westend' public house in Kensington in 1838, watched by a crowd of 3,000.

Publicans often hired cricket 'grounds' to promote events, such as the pedestrian match (walking matches) between the 'Manchester Pet' and a local east London champion on an October bank holiday in 1843. Such matches attracted huge crowds but some became so disruptive due to drinking and gambling that the authorities reduced the number of bank holidays in the 1830s and 1840s from forty a year to just four.

Any activity that might bring in customers would be encouraged and so bowling alleys and greens were often added to licensed premises. Boxing rooms were not uncommon and there is evidence of a Fives court (a form of squash played with the hand) being built onto a public house in Nottingham in 1834.

Cock-fighting was replaced by both bowling and boxing for gambling purposes. Boxing attracted punters and bookmakers alike, with bloody fistfights fought out in upstairs rooms until they too were banned.

Bowling becomes acceptable

Bowling was another unlawful rural sport that became urbanised and regulated, with the first fully documented match (the 'Knighthood Competition') held in Southampton on August 1st, 1776.

Such games grew into tournaments and were sponsored by public houses, the best known of which were held at the 'Talbot' and 'Waterloo' inns in Blackpool. Both are still held today and are sponsored by breweries and televised. This tradition continued as sportsmen retired and became publicans. So, we still have:

- boxing publicans in the East End of London
- bowling publicans in Lancashire

- wrestling publicans in Cumbria

- cricket publicans in Yorkshire

- football publicans practically everywhere.

In northeast England the 'miners' sports' of quoits, dog racing and pigeon flying are still popular with pubs and publicans just as they were in 1855 when the *Newcastle Daily Chronicle* of January 23rd featured twenty-five public houses promoting practically every known sport from rowing to quoits.

The public house was the traditional centre for many rural sports that had originated as mediaeval 'holy day' sports and this continued over succeeding centuries with:

- The Kersal Cell – Salford Sports

- The Golden Ball – Overton Sports, Lancashire

- The Bridge Inn – Ironbridge Fair, Shropshire

- The Hyde Park – Leeds Feast.

Activities were advertised as 'Old English sports' such as jumping, leaping, throwing and 'climbing the pole' and typical prizes included cheeses, pairs of boots and hats.

The growth of sporting sponsorship

The other major source of sponsorship was the nobility and the gentry who began to promote various sports for entertainment in the eighteenth century. This trend can be traced to the changing financial climate caused by, as Defoe noted, 'a prodigious conflux of nobility and gentry from all parts of England into London'.

These people financed theatres, gardens, clubs and sports through investment as well as their own gambling, spectating and participation. The prosperity created by their spending led to a revival of the ancient public schools to which the children of the 'new rich' were sent so that they might become part of the country's social and financial elite.

Aristocratic support for horse racing ensured that by the eighteenth century most sizeable towns had a racecourse and several days each year would be set aside for race meetings. Some town councils promoted these meetings as commercial ventures but their success often depended upon local nobility who provided the major prizes, as for example at:

- Stockport (1764) – Lord FitzHerbert and Lord Egerton
- Warwick (1784) – 16 local noblemen
- Lancaster (1772) – Lord Stanley and 150 gentry.

It is important to note that the racing industry provided employment to whole communities, including farriers, blacksmiths, grooms and jockeys. Winnings also generated thousands of pounds for owners in prize monies and stud fees.

Much aristocratic support was transferred to cricket, which was described in a book published in 1802 as, 'a sport formerly confined solely to the labouring classes but becoming daily more fashionable among those whose rank and fortune enable expectations of a very different conduct'.

By 1845, *Denison's Cricketers Companion* was able to produce an extensive list of noblemen 'by whom clubs are either supported or patronised'.

Whilst cricket became largely urbanised, hunting and shooting inevitably remained as rural pursuits. Also, as cricket became increasingly gentrified, hunting and shooting opened their doors to an increasing level of middle-class participation.

'Subscription hunts' were started and were open to those who could afford the annual fees and mostly hunted foxes, which had become a real pest problem in the mid-eighteenth century. Whilst many joined hunts for entertainment, the search for social and/or commercial advancement was also a high priority, in much the same way as it is for some who join golf clubs today.

Democratisation also occurred in shooting as a result of the Game Reform Bill (1831), which gave access to anybody who could afford a game certificate. This encouraged the gentry to charge for shooting on their land and caused immense resentment as 'rough shooters' were forced to pay for the first time. Many ended up in court and in jail for not having a certificate.

A 'bit of a flutter'

Gentlemen have gambled on sport from the earliest times. Organised horse racing resulted largely from a desire to gamble and this instinct passed through generations into the public school culture, where gambling and drinking were commonplace.

Wagers on horse racing were often taken by clerks of the course whose job it was to administer the financial side of the meeting to the satisfaction of the stewards (the local gentry). These clerks were sometimes less than honest and winnings were often not paid, which gave racing a bad name.

An example of this occurred at Lichfield Races in 1797, when the clerk of the course (Mr Handey) was advised by Lord Spencer and Sir Robert Williams: '... to make payment of race money into Cobb's bank and do so before he obliges them to proceed to some very unpleasant measures'.

The cock-fights staged at public houses during race weeks further indulged the gambling instincts of race-goers and wagers were often very large. Fifty guineas (£50 and 50 shillings) was wagered on every match at the Lancaster Races of 1772 and 500 guineas on one match at Warwick Races in 1827.

This gambling mania affected all sections of society but was particularly obvious amongst the leisured class who wagered huge sums on just about anything – sporting or otherwise. Below are three examples:

- Prize fighting (January 1681): The Duke of Albemarle's footman against a local 'champion' for 1,000 guineas (£100,000 today)

- Rowing (August 1765): 'The greatest wager ever rowed' for 2,000 guineas (£190,000 today)

- Cricket (September 1791): Nottinghamshire against a team of 'All-stars' for 2,000 guineas. (£195,000 today)

Prize fighting had long attracted the attention of the gentry and James Figg established himself as a 'master of the noble art of defence' at Adam and Eve Court, Oxford Road, London as early as 1719, and the gentlemen themselves began the Pugilistic Club there in 1814.

It was even common for money bouts to take place in the public schools and one such match resulted in the death of Ashley, son of Lord Shaftesbury, at Eton College in 1825 when his opponent fell on his throat and killed him. An eyewitness wrote: 'As in all prize fights, they allow a man, if his opponent falls, to tumble on him and if his knee comes down on his chest or head, so much the better'.

At the other end of the social scale there were literally thousands of local matches around the country – such as the one organised by the local publican at Whittlesford in Cambridgeshire on January 21st, 1863 between a farmer and a fisherman for £5. The farmer, who was clearly fitter than the fisherman, apparently gave his opponent 'a good punching'.

'Pedestrians'

Publicans also promoted pedestrian meetings at local running grounds that often featured regional champions such as:

- 'The Crowcatcher' from London
- 'The Gateshead Clipper'
- 'The Norwich Millboy'
- 'The Manchester Pet'
- 'Folkestone Bess'.

These events were often 'fixed' for gambling purposes, such as that at the Lillie Bridge stadium (London) in 1887, when two famous pedestrians, Harry Gent and Harry Hutchens, failed to start a race because their respective sponsors each wanted to arrange for their man to lose.

The spectators became so enraged that they rioted and burned the stadium to the ground, an act which finally decided the gentlemen of the Amateur Athletic Association to exclude professionals and 'quasi-amateurs' from the sport altogether.

Sporting enclosures

Following the effective gentrification of pedestrianism, a sport that captured the imagination of the working class was dog racing. First mentioned in *The Times* of September 11th, 1876, this sport presented another opportunity for yet more gambling.

Sports promoters knew that good crowds were vital in order to make a profit. Many gentlemen had taken the 'Grand Tour' of Europe and had been much impressed by the regattas in Venice; so much so that in 1775 they organised a similar event at on the river Thames at Chelsea, which attracted 200,000 people. The 'gentlemen' built themselves a grandstand, ensuring both their own safety and a good view but most of the crowd spent their time drinking and gambling with the result that seven of them drowned.

It was often impossible to charge entrance money at many early events since they were held in open areas. Promoters saw the enclosure of grounds as 'key' to making a profit, whilst amateur (and later professional) clubs saw that enclosing their grounds gave them control over who was admitted and a means of generating income that would ensure their continued existence.

Boundaries and other perimeters

Cricket promoters were amongst the first to realise the commercial implications of enclosing grounds and the daily *Universal Register* of the June 22nd, 1785 reported that the White Conduit Fields (London) were being enclosed for 'the security and amusement of the Lordling Cricketers' and – it might have added – their profit.

Nottingham and Sheffield also had enclosed grounds by the early nineteenth century and by 1900 most of the sixteen first-class cricket sides played to crowds in excess of 10,000. *The Times*, in 1908, suggested that the increase in income and the purchasing of better players had 'converted the game of cricket from an occasional pastime of geniality into a more or less mechanical trade'.

By 1942 the *Cricketers' Year Book* (known as *Wisden* after its publisher) noted that the commercialised game had begun to attract 'the kind of spectator not wanted at county cricket matches'. Cricket and other mass spectator sports had to choose between admitting larger, often troublesome crowds or excluding them and incurring a financial loss. By the 1980s this had become a chronic dilemma, which will be revisited in Chapter Eight.

Paddocks and other enclosures

Horse racing was heavily commercialised in the eighteenth century and increasing spectator demand encouraged promoters to provide select areas for owners and trainers and grandstands for the wealthy whilst continuing to provide cheaper enclosures for the ordinary race-goers.

The Jockey Club had provided separate facilities for its Newmarket members in the 1760s and this led to improved grandstands at places like Fulwood (Preston) in 1790 and 1805, and Newton (Lancashire) in 1824.

Subsequently the perceived commercial advantages of providing facilities for all social classes meant that between 1836 and 1846 most racing venues acquired an improved range of enclosures. Even humble amateur events such as the Bungay Steeple Chase in Suffolk in 1915 were forced to levy charges as follows:

▪ Admission to Grandstand   12/6

- Admission to Paddock   10/6
- Admission to Course   7/6
- Parking for motor cars   15/-.

Football grounds and gate money

Traditionally, football had been played on open ground where it often caused damage and disruption. So, when the game moved into urban areas, local gentlemen acted quickly to restrict it to safer and more manageable spaces. It became usual for the game to be played in areas enclosed by neighbouring yards, houses or factories and sometimes on land attached to churches.

Teams from different neighbourhoods began to play each other 'home' and 'away' and town champions would play each other, creating the league system of today.

As support (and income) grew, playing areas would be developed, with a perimeter wall and turnstiles being priorities. This allowed clubs to control entry and charge entrance fees with successful clubs becoming wealthy enough to employ semi-professional players. This increased the distinction between amateur and professional teams.

Some clubs were more successful than others in this respect. Tottenham Hotspur FC, which became a limited company in 1899, had 'a very fine enclosure that could accommodate 25,000 spectators and annual gate receipts of £6,399'. In the same year Lancaster FC optimistically had 5,000 tickets printed for a local cup match.

Even the 'gentlemanly' amateur rugby union clubs began to enclose their grounds and small clubs such as Bolton RFC used canvas sheeting to erect a grandstand and charged a 3d (1 ½p) entrance fee. Generally, rugby in the north of England followed the pattern of football and teams from working class areas soon found that by paying expenses to players, financed from gate receipts, they had jeopardised the amateur status of their players – as defined by gentlemen in the south.

As northern crowds grew, the huge gate-money income was spent on ground improvements, buying and selling players and team tours.

However, unlike the Football Association, the rugby authorities were not prepared to accept any remotely professional activity and the northerners, who had kept the word 'Union' in their breakaway movement of 1895, finally formed their own rugby 'League' in 1922. By 1929 attendances of 40,000 at rugby league's cup final were too large for any northern ground and the game was moved to Wembley Stadium, the country's largest sporting arena.

Few sports could avoid the commercial necessity of balancing the books, with annual subscriptions often being insufficient to cover expenses. One of the earliest cycling clubs, the Oken BC (Warwick), provoked much resentment among members and supporters by charging 6d for entry to its (track) matches in 1883.

The business of sport

By the mid-nineteenth century many of the mediaeval fairs held on common land had been replaced by 'sports' organised by local committees on rented fields. This meant that it became necessary to charge for entry.

This was so up and down the country and the Linton (Cambridgeshire) Sports of 1879 stipulated positively 'No free admission and no half-prices', whilst the Darlington (Co. Durham) Sports of 1920 was possible only 'due to the gate monies'.

There were those who for commercial reasons supplied the needs of sportsmen by providing facilities for the 'business of general athletic entertainments'. The Sheriff of Hull did this in 1889 when he formed an association with local cycling, athletic and cross-country clubs to form the Hull Athletic Ground Company Limited. This and similar companies elsewhere sought to construct grandstands and tracks, and provide facilities for athletic sports which would attract crowds of 20,000 and provide shareholders with substantial profits.

Spectatorism

The general trend towards spectatorism began in the eighteenth century and became obvious during World War II when the *Mass Observation Archive* noted that: 'it is a pity that the Englishmen's idea of sport is changing since it now consists mainly of being spectators rather than players'.

London was the centre of sporting (and other) activity and was where both men and their masters headed: the former to seek work and the latter in search of greater prosperity and pleasure.

Many ordinary men were engaged as servants or as hired help. Much of the pleasure enjoyed by both was in gambling on the fortunes of the former as cricketer, jockey, pedestrian, pugilist or sculler.

It is important to note that commercial influences gradually replaced the rural traditions of barter and payment in kind. The country became more urbanised, work became more sophisticated and paper money was more widely used, so it is not surprising that sport as business and spectator entertainment should have evolved from the eighteenth century onwards.

Town councils also promoted sport for commercial purposes and as early as 1698 Lancaster Races were organised to coincide with the visit of the travelling assize court. Gravesend Corporation established a regatta to support the industry of its watermen. Most local councils at that time were (not unusually) made up of the gentry and many of them mixed business with pleasure in promoting sport, particularly horse racing.

The accounts of some of the men responsible for raising and collecting race subscriptions show how successful they were in doing so. Samuel Armitage, Esq., William Horton, Esq. and John Baldwin were responsible for collecting the race subscriptions for Skircoate Moor Races near Halifax on the August 3rd, 1736. The support they managed to enlist is indicated below:

- 11 local aristocrats   @ 1 guinea
- 30 gentlemen   @ ½ guinea
- 70 tradesmen   @ 5 shillings
- 162 minor tradesmen   @ 2/6d
- 72 private individuals   @ 1 shilling

                                      Total £66.4s.0d.

Races were named after people who had donated money so we find:

- Gentlemen's Sweepstake of 100 guineas (Lichfield, 1752)
- Town Purse of £50 (Stockport, 1763)
- Noblemen's Purse of £50 (Lancaster, 1772).

Towards the end of the eighteenth century, many gentlemen withdrew their support from race meetings because of race fixing and financial irregularities. This led to some local councils facing claims for compensation.

Another way of boosting income was to increase charges to others who made commercial use of a venue. In 1829 the Fulwood Race Course Company raised the rent of the refreshment area in the Ladies' Stand from £7 to £20 and decided that 'all stake and basket people and all tents and booths were to pay £5'.

Commercialism

Despite the efforts of public school-educated administrators, commercialism in sport grew and even the Stewards of the Henley Royal Regatta considered allowing 'minstrels and comic singers' to perform at their event to improve profits.

Cricket also became big business and the personal support of clubs like Hambledon gradually gave way to private professional cricket tours promoted by such men as Arthur Shaw of Nottingham and James Lillywhite of Sussex, which regularly made profits of £20,000 to £25,000. Profits, however, were not guaranteed and Miss Agnes Rowley of the Lady Cricketers took a Mr Wood to court in 1892 to secure payment of £11 for a failed tour of the provinces.

In boxing, the era of the household servant being retained by his master gave way to the pure entertainment of James Burke, the All-England champion in the 1840s, who dressed as a clown in the ring and played in pantomime out of it.

Boxing evolved into a businesslike exploitation in the late nineteenth century, with promoters such as Martin Lane in Manchester who took Billy Marchant from the fairground boxing booths and made him into a champion. Boxing grew in popularity in Manchester, as it did elsewhere, and another promoter, Jack Smith, attracted large audiences and top London fighters to its biggest venue, the Free Trade Hall.

Also in Manchester, athletics changed from the simple rural sports of Kersal Moor to promotions of 'Monster Athletic Fêtes' at Pomona Palace – held to promote the opening of Manchester Town Hall in 1877. In the above case a 'variety of old English sports' was augmented with a large programme of events for money prizes.

Another promoter, Harry Hardwick, established the Northern Cross Country Association (NCCA) in 1882 and used the Manchester racecourse for championships. By 1888, athletic meetings were held at Belle Vue before crowds of 10,000 but their popularity waned in the 1920s due to rival attractions such as football and hiking.

The commercial aspects of athletics promotion were high on the agenda of the fledgling Olympic Games almost from the outset and by 1904 (St Louis) the business influence of the World Fair Movement, which was used to sponsor the

Olympics was already undermining its ideals. This will be revisited in Chapter Nine.

Other sports pursued financial viability with golf clubs advertising charges for visiting players and the Professional Golfers Association seeking sponsorship deals for its championships. Fishing clubs arranged permits for holidaymakers and, with rowing clubs, negotiated preferential seaside excursion rates with the railway companies. Swimming clubs also promoted displays by professional swimmers.

Such levels of commercialisation led to the growth of a sports industry as businessmen exploited the growing market for recreational invention and innovation.

Horse racing had long been associated with gambling, and during the nineteenth century, Tattersalls and others began to develop this potential. Horse breeding and sales soon became big business and the *Racing Calendar*, first published in 1811, was a shop window for the industry in all its forms. Edition No. 1 of April 4th of that year featured the following:

- 70 horses for sale at a total of 8,000 guineas
- 125 horses at stud with fees of 14,400 guineas
- 15 race meetings in two months.

Apart from the *Sporting Calendar* there were also:

- *The Sportsman*
- *Sporting Life*
- *The Sporting Chronicle*.

All of the above sold 300,000 copies per day during the late Victorian period.

Although the practice of racing dogs after hares (coursing) was relatively minor, it shadowed horse racing as a commercial business and attracted a similar gambling fraternity as well as sponsorship and sales of animals. It evolved into the highly organised urban sport of greyhound racing at tracks such as Belle Vue in Manchester, built in 1926 at a cost of £25,000.

The football 'industry'

The game of football had attained 'industry status' well before the twentieth century with a trade union established in 1898 to represent players' interests to the club owners. Players were then legally owned assets and were simply bought and sold, often just to turn a quick profit.

Mercer of Hull City was bought for £40 in 1919 but sold in 1921 for £4,000.

Meehan of Manchester United was sold for a profit of £3,000 in the same year.

Neither man apparently had any desire to leave their homes or clubs.

The Professional Footballers Union report of 1945 severely criticised owners, chairmen and administrators for not providing greater security for players. Such criticism is still voiced today although in rather different circumstances.

Both football and racing attained enormous popularity between the wars due partly to coverage in the sporting press and on the radio, which was to be found in 71 per cent of households by 1939.

The influence of tennis and cycling

Tennis had originally been played in monasteries and adapted for their exclusive use by the aristocracy.

It also had its rustic version, born out of the habit of the lower orders of mimicking the pastimes of their 'betters'. This latter game evolved into field tennis and eventually became lawn tennis when it was marketed by Major Wingfield to be played in the privacy of middle-class suburban gardens.

Henry Jones, a founder member of the Wimbledon Croquet Club, saw the potential of tennis, which came to dominate the club's activities to such an extent that the Wimbledon Championship is now one of the premier sporting occasions of the world and an industry in itself.

It was the growth of the commercial appeal of tennis, as well as other aspects of social change, that transformed the way in which women dressed – and were portrayed by the media.

Although (like lawn tennis) the full commercial potential of athletics was not to be fully realised until the arrival of the television era, we can see that its business potential was fully understood more than a century ago by reading prospectuses such as that of the Hull Athletic Ground Company (1889), which declared that its intention was 'to carry on any business calculated to benefit the company financially' and that it would 'employ professional men qualified for their work who have made this class of business their special pursuit'.

Similarly, the development of the running shoe began more than a century ago with Joseph William Foster, a member of the Bolton Primrose Harriers, producing 'Foster's Shoes' in 1900. Many years later this business evolved into Reebok UK, which sells millions of shoes throughout the world and was bought by Adidas in 2006.

'Foster's Shoes' were also bought by an increasing number of cyclists who were encouraged onto the roads by new and improved bicycles.

The finest of these machines was James Starley's safety bicycle of 1886, which was the first to enjoy huge nationwide sales and which no doubt contributed to the fact that by the end of the nineteenth century there were over 500 cycling clubs in England.

The bicycle provided freedom from the urban environment for countless millions of people, particularly women, many of whom took the first opportunity to grasp a degree of personal independence in a male dominated world.

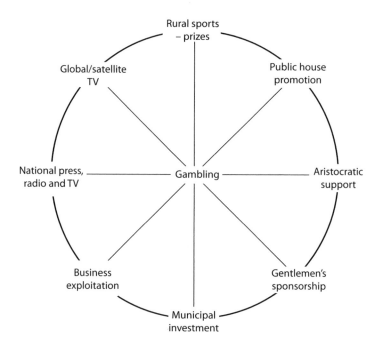

FIGURE 3.1   The evolution of commercialisation

Common themes

Commercialism has always been present in sport in one form or another. It may have begun with the donation of prizes by local tradesmen at holy day recreations and have become more highly organised in rural sports, often sponsored by publicans.

Gentry patronage was evident in the eighteenth century along with promotion by municipal authorities, both of which led to an increase in gambling and spectatorism. Event organisers sought further commercial development and this exploitation of the commercial potential of sport is only beginning to reach its full extent in today's age of global communication.

A major effect of the commercialisation of sport was the growth of professionalism and this topic is the subject of the next chapter.

QUESTIONS

THE COMMERCIALISATION OF SPORT

1 Explain the role of the gentry in prize-fighting and pedestrianism.

2 Discuss the reasons for the development of sporting enclosures.

3 Why were issues of professionalism found in predominantly industrial areas?

4 The building of grandstands reflected both commercialism and class division. Explain this.

Suggested further reading

Golby, J. and Purdue, A., *The Civilisation of the Crowd: Popular Culture in England 1750–1900* (Batsford, 1984)

Malcolmson, R., *Popular Recreations in English Society 1700–1850* (Cambridge University Press, 1973)

Plumb, J., *The Commercialisation of Leisure in the Eighteenth Century* (Reading University Press, 1974)

chapter four

PROFESSIONALISM

The professional takes pleasure in his business and is generally a capital fellow whose only failing is to spend improvidently what he earns easily.

(The Times, *May 20th, 1882*)

The idea of receiving money for winning sporting contests dates from at least the sixth century when Solon decreed that any Athenian gaining victory at the Olympic Games should be paid 600 drachmae.

By the beginning of the nineteenth century the threefold influence of rural sports, gentlemen's patronage and commercial exploitation had produced a class of competitor who was able to derive financial benefit from a number of sporting activities.

In pedestrianism for example, the notion of prize winning originated in mediaeval times when food, drink or clothing were awarded to victors. Pedestrian 'matches' were later organised for large sums in both prize funds and wagers.

At small local sports up and down the country it was common for the men's races to be run for money prizes and this continues today. The major games provided substantial prize funds for what were 'amateur' events and this went on despite huge efforts by the sport's governing body (run by gentlemen) to put an end to it.

With the revival of the Olympic Games in 1896, the concept of strict amateurism was soon challenged and inducements in kind were offered in the games of 1906 when the Greek winner of the marathon won free food for a year at his local restaurant.

The manufacture of equipment, particularly shoes, soon became an important factor and makers began to pay 'expenses' to the better athletes so that their products received greater media coverage. Gradually, as financial inducements grew larger, winning became the whole purpose of competition and a nation's prestige depended on the success or otherwise of its athletes. As a result, 'professional attitudes' were encouraged by governing bodies fearing international humiliation.

Prizes make professionals

The Morpeth Olympic Games in Northumberland had been fully professional since 1874 when £7 had been the prize for the premier race (a sum that had risen to £75 by 1925). So popular was this meeting that a new track was laid in 1921 and total prize money rose to £340, making the event second to none in the country.

Cash prizes were common in the north of England, not only for athletic events but also for flower shows and brass band contests. Winners were not considered to have lost their amateur status but this was not so in the south, where they were known as 'quasi-amateurs'.

The prospectus for the Hull Athletic Ground Company (1889) makes it clear that an essential component of its activity was 'to offer sums of money for prizes for the purpose of encouraging sports and athletics generally'.

Even in the south of England, where the sums of money were usually smaller, the tradition of cash prizes was well established so that small events like the Sutton and Linton Sports (Cambs.) gave money prizes for all their events.

Such events had grown over centuries from rural sports where some material payment for winning had been considered normal simply because ordinary people were often in desperate need of food or clothing.

Wrestling and boxing, two of the very oldest rural sports, maintained their popularity with the labouring classes. Wrestling was very popular in the remote areas of Cumberland and Cornwall, whilst boxing flourished in the urban areas of the north and midlands and in the booths of travelling fairs all over the country.

Cumbrians regarded wrestling as the king of sports and it was also the chief outlet for displays of physical fitness and training. Huge contests were staged at Carlisle, Keswick, Penrith and Whitehaven, drawing the cream of wrestlers from all over the region. One champion, Richard Chapman of Patterdale, was a policeman who became landlord of the Ship Inn at Maryport during the 1830s where he continued to promote and umpire the sport.

Although Cumberland wrestling had been common in the seventeenth and eighteenth centuries at fairs, it was not until the early nineteenth century that it became a major attraction with thousands of spectators attending the major centres where bouts were fought for substantial sums of money.

'Fixing and fouling'

Promoters were well aware that fights were 'fixed' by competitors and a poster advertising a match at Penrith on July 18th, 1863 warned that, 'any man known to receive or make a bribe or make a "sham wrestle" will be excluded from the Penrith ring and his offence communicated to every ring in the country'.

By the nineteenth century, boxing (prize fighting) had become wholly professional but despite the *London Prize Ring Rules* of 1838 it continued to be disreputable as fighters disregarded rules in pursuit of big money prizes.

Leading fighters were seen to 'fix and foul' bouts to the disgust of those who risked money on them. Gentleman backers withdrew into their own clubs where the sport could be properly controlled. This was exemplified by a bout between William Thompson and Ben Caunt in 1843 in which blatantly low punching caused Thompson to lose in the seventy-fifth round.

Thompson, a typical fighter from a large family (of twenty-one children), escaped the workhouse by fighting for a pittance, often in secret, on canal barges, river steamers, backyards and isolated fields. Such men often built a reputation which led to bigger 'prize matches' and championship bouts.

It seems that economic depressions produce new fighters. The great depression of the late 1920s/early 1930s produced so many that the British Boxing Board of Control (1929) was established to protect them from too much damage or financial exploitation. Even in 1992 the Professional Boxers' Association was formed to protect the interests of another influx of fighters – for exactly similar reasons!

Professionalism and the 'great divide'

Such activities always attracted the poor as means of survival and maybe considerable wealth.

Some of the original *bruisers* were Thames watermen who rowed one-ton wherries up and down river all day. They understood the concept of payment for success having been sponsored to row races since the end of the seventeenth century, including the Doggett Coat and Badge Race from 1715 onwards.

This grew out of the practice of bonus payments for speedy journeys – much as one might offer a tip to a taxi driver for getting you to an appointment on time. The commonplace nature of wager racing is evident from reports in *The Aquatic Register* for the period 1835–51, which records 5,000 such races occurring at the rate of around five per week.

Professional oarsmen were used to:

- act as trainers to amateur clubs
- row in wager races for gentlemen
- make up joint crews with gentlemen.

More commonly, professional crews were backed for large sums of money – such as the £300 wagered between Captain Rose and Squire Osbaldston whose crews rowed round a yacht in Brighton harbour in 1830.

Several rowing personalities gained national and international status and in the rowing heartland of the River Tyne they were treated like heroes. Some indication of the importance of boat racing on the Tyne lies in a description of a race day published in 1873:

> **When a professional sculling race comes off the heart of the town is convulsed, the stations teem with unfamiliar forms and faces. The river steamers groan, the cart wheels rattle over the granite roads, the sound of the forge dies away, the blast of the furnaces is unheard, the counting house and desk are deserted and the academic benches are vacant and all hasten to the banks of the coaly Tyne, the radical and the tory, master and servants, the great white washed and the great unwashed, every available elevation clad with living forms. Such conveys only a faint idea of the feelings that animate every breast.**

By the way, Squire Osbaldston was interested in many sports outside his own preference of hunting and was heavily involved in promoting cricket, notably the Sussex team for which he sometimes played and frequently gambled on, losing 300 guineas on one occasion.

Gentlemen and players

In cricket, as in rowing, gentry' patronage positively encouraged the growth of professionalism and in a retrospective assessment written in 1909, Lord Harris

maintained that: 'After two centuries of comradeship on the field, there is no need to encourage disputations on the definition of amateur'.

At that time, there were many 'disputations' in sports such as athletics and rugby union but cricket continued to treat its professionals like the servants of old and provided some financial aid to them during the off-season to ensure their welfare.

In the north of England, where amateurs and professionals were socially more compatible, Lord Hawke of the Yorkshire CCC (County Cricket Club) had for years organised payment of 'talent money' for success on the field and established a fund into which bonus money was paid during the season. This was then divided up between the professional players.

The Marylebone Cricket Club (MCC) treated its professionals even more like servants, employing them exclusively for the purpose of 'bowling at the gentlemen batsmen for practice'.

Less prestigious clubs followed the MCC's example and employed professionals to help them practise and to lead the bowling in matches. So we find references in club minute books that 'servants and bowlers' had been appointed.

In 1863, the Worksop Cricket Club devoted 'all annual subscriptions to engage a professional bowler' and this became so common that by the middle of the nineteenth century most clubs in the country had at least one paid professional.

The accounts of many of these clubs show that the wages of the professionals and the bonus monies made up the greatest single expense and required clubs to continue the pursuit of commercialism in order to make ends meet.

Even the Gloucestershire County Cricket Club was in financial difficulties – caused largely by payments of £4.10s.00d for each player and £15 for W.G. Grace for every match in which he played. Grace was probably worth it since people flocked to watch him play wherever they were in the country. In 1879 the payments were reduced to 'expenses only' – except for Dr Grace, of course, whose 'special commercial attraction' was recognised.

The distinction between amateurs and professionals in cricket remained until 1962 when the game became 'open' but even then the gentlemen continued to be critical and *Wisden* commented that: 'by doing away with amateurs cricket is in danger of losing the spirit and freedom of the best amateurs and could have detrimental effects in the vital matters of captaincy at county and test levels'.

Matters concerning amateurism and professionalism varied from one sport to another and were looked upon differently in the north and the south. Cricket had always accepted professionals so that Grace's strange role as a 'so-called amateur' was tolerated far more readily than would have been the case in some other sports.

Before turning to the situation in rugby union we should note that everywhere in the country it was common for sporting associations to employ servants; so that, for instance, we find:

- Huntsmen and 'whips' in fox hunting
- Ground staff at bowling clubs
- Caddies and caddy master at golf clubs
- Instructors at swimming clubs etc.

'Broken time'

As we have seen, the Rugby Football Union was completely against any form of payment to players irrespective of whether this was compensation for wages lost whilst playing, for travelling or other expenses or even simple gifts.

In the north all these means had been used to pay players so that it became inevitable that the northerners should establish their own governing body. This they did at a meeting at the George Hotel, Huddersfield on August 29th, 1895.

The new Northern Rugby Football Union pledged to pay players only to compensate for lost wages or 'for bona fide broken time' and stated that they repudiated any idea of professionalism and 'will punish strictly any departure from this principle'.

Unfortunately, there were so many 'departures' that it proved impossible to enforce and in 1900 the NRFU sanctioned the existence of a professional class by stipulating on May 1st of that year that 'clubs shall only be able to register players as professional who are in receipt of actual payments for playing football'.

Even so, very few were full-time professionals since most kept their jobs and played rugby part-time. They were, however, vilified by the 'gentlemen' in the south as the enemies of true sport. In reality they were ordinary working folk who enjoyed playing sport, were good at it and sought to supplement a meagre income with small sums of sorely needed cash.

Nevertheless, the NRFU endeavoured to minimise the spread of professionalism by fining clubs who tried to 'poach' players. We find comments in minute books noting '... that the Holbeck club be fined £20 for inducing W. Carey, a professional from the Leeds Parish Church Club, to sign professional forms for them'. Carey was also suspended from playing for a month.

The southern gentlemen did not really understand the financial plight of northern workers who might have a family of ten to feed on a week's wage of eighteen shillings (90 pence). This, as a speaker at a sportsmen's dinner in 1866 said, was what many gentlemen would spend on one meal.

These difficulties were more generally recognised in cricket where the employment situation had evolved from the traditional master/servant relationship and regular 'benefit' matches were held to raise money for players' retirements. One such was the match for George Parr, a loyal servant of the Marylebone club, who received several thousand pounds from a crowd of 6,000 people in 1858.

The situation in the north was very different. Entrance charges were lower, as were sporting wages, which meant that players kept their ordinary jobs or worked seasonally.

The professionals stand their ground

The end of the nineteenth century saw the onset of full-time professionalism. This was due to the growth of the league system of competition, which guaranteed well-attended matches throughout a long season.

The growing popularity of the league system in both football codes in the north of England led to the formation of the Lancashire Cricket League in 1892. This league encouraged the employment of professionals by all the participating clubs in pursuit of competitive (and therefore commercial) success.

The clubs arranged matches so that working people could watch on Saturday afternoons and the professional would be employed to coach the amateurs and generally develop the club's performance whilst also playing and attracting the paying customers.

Payment in the Lancashire and Yorkshire leagues was usually for the whole season with bonuses for performance and improved gate receipts. Elsewhere it was often payment per match or number of matches, as was the case at Whitfield Cricket Club in Northumberland where the professional was paid £51 for ten matches.

'Acceptable professionals'

The distinction between amateurs and professionals in cricket became increasingly blurred as more players were paid. Some were paid directly and others indirectly by being given expenses. It is not unusual to find, as with Bolton Cricket Club in 1937, that every player received some form of income with the season's wage bill totalling £265.

The Yorkshire clubs' idea of 'merit marks' awarded for good conduct and skill became widely adopted. This was usually based on five shillings (25 pence) being earned for every merit mark awarded and was paid to players at the end of the season.

Whilst cricket assimilated 'paid players' into its ranks relatively painlessly, association football struggled to try and exclude them but failed. Payments were made and teams that were professional in all but name flourished competitively and commercially in the north and midlands.

In 1885 the Football Association was forced to recognise this and allowed payment of wages to players. This was a move which far from setting up a free market in football had the effect of binding players to one club and setting a maximum wage. Rule 18 of the new code introduced in 1890 forbade players from joining another club without their club's consent and this restriction, together with the low maximum wage, encouraged players to form a union, which they did in 1898.

This became the Football Players Association (FPA) in 1907 and was established 'to provide legal advice in connection with professional engagements including claims under the Workmen's Compensation Act of 1906'.

The FPA immediately but unsuccessfully tried to have the maximum wage abolished and the level of opposition to such a move can be gauged from the fact that this did not happen until 1961 with freedom of transfer not granted until 1963.

Despite these difficulties, the 'people's game' went from strength to strength and by 1911, 34 of the 36 towns with populations of 100,000 or more had professional teams, many of which were substantial businesses.

In 1915, Tottenham Hotspur FC was paying out £3,940 in wages and by retaining its best players and engaging some of the best available at that time the club looked forward to its first season in the first division. The club had weathered the financial storm caused by the declining gates of the 1914–18 war and by 1933 it had an income of £52,192.

Some other clubs paid players throughout the war but the Leeds City club was subsequently expelled from the league for making illegal payments. This resulted in the formation of Leeds United at Elland Road in 1920.

Few sports resisted the move towards professionalism, even those mainly middle-class sports such as tennis, cycling and golf. The Wimbledon Championships had become so successful even before World War I that special trains took thousands to the finals and the better foreign players received legitimate expenses as they were deemed to be representing their countries.

It gradually became impossible for tennis to remain amateur at the highest level. Clubs employed professionals as trainers and coaches but as soon as they could be well paid in championships abroad, they left in order to make more money.

The Wimbledon committee discussed admitting professionals in 1935 but decided against it by a large majority. It was not until 1967 that the championships finally became 'open'.

Bicycling: sport and business

Technical advances in bicycle manufacture towards the end of the nineteenth century had improved the quality and availability of bicycles so that by 1900 there were some 700 factories producing huge numbers of bicycles that were within the reach of ordinary people to use for transport and for recreation. Consequently cycling grew from being a middle-class activity to one of mass participation.

Much of the early competition in cycling had been time-trialling on public roads but professional track racing had begun in France and was taken up in England with the first such event held in Fulham in 1871. This was so successful that promoters also built tracks in Bristol, Coventry, London and Manchester, which popularised the sport even further.

The initial middle-class interest in cycling waned as a reaction to the democratisation of the sport, which saw an increasing number of ordinary working people taking part for both recreation and as a sport. Partly as a consequence of this, many former cyclists began to buy motorcycles and motorcars as they became fashionable.

Although it was popular in the UK, professional cycling never matched the huge following it gained in Europe. However, several clubs in the north of England did prosper and their better cyclists took part in semi-professional events around the northern region. The Darlington club, for example, provided prizes of 7 guineas and 5 guineas for their championships in 1927. The very best performers turned fully professional after World War II but competed mostly abroad.

Cycling too had its 'issues' which were focused not only on the question of competing for money but on whether racing should be confined to enclosed tracks or permitted on the open road.

A number of organisations, including the National Cyclists Union (1883) and the Road Racing Council (1922), took different views on such matters.

It was not until 1959 that the present British Cycling Federation was formed from an amalgamation of existing organisations. Clearly these difficulties may have influenced the development of cycling as a sport in the UK.

Golf too...

Like cricket, golf too began as a classless activity but was gentrified during the nineteenth century when the gulf between gentlemen and players and club members and professionals first appeared.

The first full-time golf professionals were hired to teach amateur members just as in cricket, rowing and tennis, and often doubled as groundsmen, handymen or caddie masters. As competition intensified, less time was spent teaching and more time playing in tournaments around the country.

This was especially so after 1857 when the first professional competition was held at Prestwick Golf Club. This evolved into the first 'open' championship (1861) where amateurs played alongside professionals and set the pattern for the development of the game both in England and abroad.

Since the mid-nineteenth century, golf has continually expanded and adjusted to meet contemporary conditions with the amateur game flourishing and the professional game prospering in the commercial glare of international tournaments. The two continue to be linked by the 'club' professional who still teaches amateur members but occasionally takes part in local professional championships.

All the sports mentioned in this book have benefited from technological innovation. Equipment has improved immeasurably over the last two centuries and continues to do so. Much of this innovation is the result of experimentation by professionals in their search for winning performances which is commercially exploited to provide the best equipment for the amateur.

The early sporting 'stars'

This improvement in the status of sport in society was promoted by a cult of personality, which was exploited by the mass circulation newspapers and reflected in popular culture.

The earliest sporting personalities were those of the pre-commercial competitions. These were men like Phelps and Broughton of the early Doggett Coat and Badge Races who were replaced in the early nineteenth century by such men as Noulton and Parish, both cunning steersmen employed by the first gentlemen's clubs. Later, also in rowing, we find the professional 'personalities' such as Robert Chambers, Harry Clasper and James Renforth whose exploits became the stuff of legend.

In cricket, the first 'personality' was John Nyren of the Hambledon Club in the 1760s, followed in the 1840s by Alfred Mynn (the Lion of Kent) and Fred Lillywhite of Sussex. All the above were totally overshadowed by W.G. Grace, whose fame extended through the last three decades of the nineteenth century. Some of his magic rubbed off on Jack Hobbs of Surrey and Herbert Sutcliffe of Yorkshire who both enjoyed mass adulation during the 1920s and the 1930s.

Many early football 'stars' were known only in their own locality but prime among them were Sam Hardy of Aston Villa and Billy Meredith of Manchester United (1880s), and Viv Woodward of Tottenham Hotspur (1900s). In rugby league men like John Anderton (Leigh), Fred Houghton (Runcorn) and Joe Varley (Oldham) also captured people's imagination.

Although athletics remained a relatively minor sport until the arrival of the television age, the first professionals, including the 'Manchester Pet' and 'Folkestone Bess', certainly attained cult status. Harold Hutchens and John Gent enjoyed similar status in the 1880s but tarnished their image by 'fixing' the race at Lillie Bridge stadium in 1887.

It should be noted that track and field athletics, rowing and rugby union were amongst the most vigorous defenders of amateur sport. Each was especially active in excluding professionals.

Early pugilists derived fame from 'fixing and fouling' but the first personalities were James Figg and Jack Broughton, who spent much energy advertising themselves and their protégés and paved the way for 'stars' such as Daniel Mendoza and 'Gentleman' John Jackson in the 1790s.

John Gully had his first fight in 1805 and had become an MP by 1832. Tom Sayers in the 1860s and Bob FitzSimmons in the 1890s were Gully's heirs but they had no real successors until the age of television.

In wrestling the national figure was Eugen Sandow who fought during the latter half of the nineteenth century but made his fortune as a strong man, performing in music halls.

The degree to which ordinary people were emotionally involved with sporting personalities can be gauged by news reports on their deaths. Fred Archer, the jockey, died tragically young and *The Times* saw this as producing 'a sense of shock and personal loss to millions'. The death of James Renforth, the world champion oarsman, was also noted in *The Newcastle Chronicle* as having produced a 'general astonishment that turned to the stupor of genuine sorrow'. The funerals of such heroes often brought hundreds of thousands of people onto the streets.

Professional personalities were often invited to amateur clubs for testimonial matches and exhibitions designed to promote the club and boost membership. Some examples of this include:

- 1865 – Harry Clasper and John Chambers (York Regatta)
- 1877 – Joe Dixon and James Walshaw (Tyldesley Swimming Club)
- 1890 – James Kay (Headingley Bowling Club)
- 1913 – Harry Vardon and Edward Ray (Lancaster Golf Club).

Such appearances earned some money but not enough to provide a living. Most professionals depended on basic weekly wages, supplemented by prizes, gambling incomes, sponsorship, tuition fees and benefits in cash and kind.

Due to a lack of recorded evidence it is impossible to evaluate precisely the income of the early professional sportsmen but by referring to reported winnings and some known wages it is possible to form some impression of what they earned. It is important to remember, however, that few professionals would continue at first class level for more than 20 years:

- bowling: £560 per championship; £50 per match
- boxing: 200–500 guineas per championship up to £3,000 for a career testimonial
- cricket: £1–£5 per match; (W.G. Grace received £15 and/or £25 per month)
- football: £2.10s.00d–£5 per week; expenses and/or transfer fees
- golf: two shillings (10p) per hour for tuition; £25 per match or exhibition

- horse racing: (an average of the most successful riders, 1870–1914) a thirty-year career might bring £75,000

- pedestrianism: £500 per championship; £50 per match

- rowing: £2 per week, plus accommodation; £30 per match (James Renforth made £2,590 in his short career)

- rugby league: £2–£5 per match.

Real success stories were relatively few. For every hero there were dozens of destitute failures who had spent what they had earned far too easily. However, there were others such as Robert Nickson, the champion bowler, who moved to the Talbot public house in Blackpool in 1873 and remained well respected and comfortably off: a continuing tradition.

In conclusion

Professionalism originated in the old rural sports where those who were good enough could win prizes in kind. This developed through noble patronage and commercial sponsorship to produce full-time professional sportsmen.

These traditions also produced folk heroes, national and international championships and a level of interest that sold hundreds of thousands of newspapers daily and brought cities to a standstill.

TABLE 4.1   The evolution of professionalism

Era	Activity/venue	Remuneration
12th to 15th century	rural sports	clothes and food
16th century	fairs and markets	small money payments
17th century	wager matches	gambling income
18th century	sponsorship by gentlemen	wages; prize funds
19th century	commercial exploitation	gambling income; prize funds; profit-share
20th century	full-time playing	wages; match-fees; appearance money;advertising revenue; contract fees; television fees
21st century	media sport	appearance money; merchandising revenue

It is difficult to believe that a profession with only some 2,500 full-time exponents in 1900 could be so influential but it was quite sufficient to produce a positive reaction from the gentleman amateur.

Gradually but with growing urgency, 'amateur' sportsmen began to distance themselves from professionalism by concentrating solely on recreational activity and by withdrawing into strictly amateur clubs.

The next chapter deals with the growth of recreationalism as a prelude to a discussion of amateur clubs.

QUESTIONS

PROFESSIONALISM

1 Why was professionalism more commonplace in the midlands and the north of England?

2 Explain the practice of 'fixing and fouling'.

3 Explain the relationship between professionalism and poverty.

4 Explain the great rift (divide) between Gentlemen and players.

5 Why do you think that professionals were readily accepted in some sports (e.g. cricket and golf) but not in others?

6 Why do you think the FA was less successful in combating the advance of professionalism than the RFU?

Suggested further reading

Brailsford, D., *Some Factors in the Evolution of Sport* (Lutterworth Press, 1993)
Marshall, M., *Gentlemen and Players* (Grafton, 1987)
Walvin, J., *The People's Game: A Social History of British Football* (Arrow Books, 1975)

chapter five

RECREATIONALISM

Every bowler exerted his abilities and the winner was declared after which they adjourned to the Half Moon where the evening concluded in the utmost harmony.

(Hampshire Chronicle, *August 4th, 1777*)

Provision should be made for the healthy and innocent recreation of all classes of people and it is proposed to establish a society for the practice of cricket, quoits, archery and other games. All classes are invited to attend.

(*Public notice in advance of the meeting, Guildhall, Walsall, June 2nd, 1846*)

Whilst commercialism and professionalism dominated sport throughout the period, recreational sport continued to minimise the importance of competition and encouraged people to take part for pleasure alone.

During the eighteenth century there had been civil disturbances around the country based on grievances to do with wages, elections, religion, enclosures and food, and most towns of any size experienced some degree of rioting or civil unrest.

Consequently, the militia was garrisoned in some forty-three towns around the country, the officers of which were responsible for establishing many sports clubs and events.

Accordingly we find particularly cricket, shooting and rowing matches in towns such as Norwich, Woolwich, Dover and Berwick which led to the eventual inauguration of local clubs.

Elsewhere the commercial middle class took its leisure in similar, if less strenuous, ways, with women boating and men playing cricket and bowls. These activities soon became the staple recreational diet of this social group.

Even so, some people did take their recreation very seriously. One Edward Grimston kept a cricket diary showing that in 1824 he had played 55 matches – or twice a week for six months. For other social groups, cock fighting (although outlawed) continued to be found in the backyards of inns, primarily for the purpose of gambling.

Boxing and wrestling matches also maintained their popularity, initially also in inn-yards but later in more established venues such as the Agricultural Hall in Islington, London.

As the mercantile class of the eighteenth century became the middle class of the nineteenth with a million more families than before, opportunities for leisure grew with increasing prosperity and free time, particularly in the wealthier south-east of the country.

'Badges of social superiority'

Much of the recreational activity can be seen as advertising this prosperity, in the same way that the gentlemen of the seventeenth century had used their recreations as 'badges of social superiority over the lower orders'. An outward manifestation of this was the uniforms chosen by club members, some examples of which included:

- The Lambton Tally-ho Club (1790) who used scarlet coats, white waistcoats and scarlet hats

- The Staffordshire Bowmen (1791) who dressed in green frock coats, white waistcoats, white trousers and dark fur hats.

- The Dresden Boat Club (1839) who expected its members to wear a blue jacket, broad brimmed straw hat and white neck-tie.

These uniforms helped to advertise the social superiority of their wearers and were further formalised in the public schools where fines were levied for 'improper dress'. When boys went up to Oxbridge they took this dress affectation into sports clubs and having been thus endorsed it found its way into the clubs formed when Oxbridge men returned to their home towns.

Recreational activity provided a good basis for business and 'networking' and participation levels grew enormously in:

- boating
- bowling
- cricket
- croquet
- fishing
- golf
- hunting
- lawn tennis
- shooting
- soccer.

The demand for boats on the Thames rocketed towards the end of the century and rowing tours from Oxford to London became the height of fashion. Records show that in 1898 10,482 pleasure boats were registered and there were similar trends at Huntingdon, Gloucester and Lincoln.

Broader recreational provision

With the expansion of middle-class activity came moves to provide recreational facilities for the less prosperous at club, municipal and works level as various philanthropists sponsored or subsidised different sports.

In 1863 Joseph Garside in Worksop provided a cricket ground for a new club which then received further 'public and private' help to lay the turf for the wicket. On the Isle of Dogs in east London, individual sponsorship and help from the church saw 'admirers of muscular Christianity [the coming together of a healthy moral (religious) mind in a physically fit body] take up boat racing, athletic sports and play in brass bands', whilst other church groups began walking tours, rail excursions and choral societies.

Titus Salt, a wealthy Bradford mill owner, provided a number of recreational facilities in his model industrial village of Saltaire – the motto of which was 'Abandon drink all ye who enter here'. In all, there were ten societies including those for boating, cricket and bowls so that in the words of a contemporary travel guide, 'mill workers from Saltaire and Shipley or shopmen and lasses could have a good day out'.

Similar philanthropy saw the new Manchester Ship Canal Company purchase Trafford Park and develop it as a golf course and boating lake in 1896. Meanwhile, town councils began providing recreational facilities in their urban redevelopment schemes. This included 'pleasure grounds', the first of which appeared at Birkenhead in 1845 and was followed by others at Leeds in 1861, Birmingham in 1869 and Newark in 1884. The tourism potential of such facilities was fully realised at places like Talkin Tarn near Carlisle and Hollingworth Lake near Rochdale, where boating, dancing, bowling and archery were catered for in the 1870s.

Many other employers in addition to Titus Salt made extensive recreational provision for their workforce. The famous confectionery firms of Cadbury's, Fry's and Rowntrees (all Quakers) laid out extensive fields and provided swimming pools, gymnasia and extensive medical facilities for their employees.

Recreational play for the masses was not always welcome and the increasingly commercialised game of football continued to be the game of the street where its capacity to cause mayhem was undiminished.

There were probably many letters similar to that penned to the clerk of Bicester Town Council on March 6th, 1899 complaining about the 'intolerable nuisance of footballing boys making their goals from lamposts and lumping against the thin walls of the houses'. This kind of behaviour was less acceptable as the nineteenth century progressed and Victorian rational and scientific philosophy was applied to society, its recreations and physical education by means of:

- increasingly severe bye-laws
- new sanitary and health reforms
- the democratisation of schooling.

Sport was included in the state school curriculum for the first time and facilities for games were provided in most towns.

Fitness becomes important

The trend towards physical fitness was accelerated by the poor standards of physical fitness discovered by the army during recruitment for the Boer War. Of the 10,000 men volunteering for service in Manchester in October 1899, 8,000 were found to be unfit for service and only 1,000 had even a moderate standard of physical fitness.

The Great War and its aftermath caused further inevitable decline, and so the government established the National Playing Fields Association (NPFA) in 1925 with a view to improving the nation's health. The emphasis was placed on the provision of 'more playing fields, playgrounds and open spaces for locals and their children'.

Not surprisingly, industrialised areas had more ill-health and fewer recreational facilities than elsewhere and were the first to form NPFA branch associations. Many of these branch associations echoed the feeling of the one in Bolton that 'there is much need for playing fields, especially for the purpose of organised games'.

The idea of rational recreation and even a proper philosophy of recreation was very largely the result of three factors:

- the growth of awareness in the therapeutic effect of exercise
- the need to create higher levels of fitness in society
- the increasing prestige of international sporting performance.

During the 1930s there was a growth in 'Keep Fit' classes, which were designed to produce 'a race of splendid men and women with fit and beautiful bodies and lively, daring minds'. The government nurtured this new athleticism by creating the National Fitness Council in 1937 and the National Advisory Council for Physical Training, which funded several full-time organisers for sport, the first of which was for amateur boxing.

Recreation and mobility

Post-war recreational activity was greatly boosted by the motorcar and it represented as much of a transport revolution in the twentieth century as rail travel had done in the nineteenth. The railways had provided an initial access to sporting activity in the 1830s when lines first connected London, Birmingham, Manchester and Newcastle.

Clearly some activities could not have taken place without rail travel, which introduced a speed and convenience not previously possible. It rendered, as Lord Greville put it on his way to Liverpool races in 1837, 'all other travelling irksome and tedious by comparison'.

Rail travel enabled increased levels of participation in sport. It encouraged City of London workers to visit their clubs in the evenings as well as at weekends, so we find in the Thames Rowing Club minutes (1861): 'the rowing train leaves Waterloo at 6.34pm and crews will be formed at 7pm'. It also had the effect of democratising travel so that all social classes (in separate compartments) could enjoy their sporting interests in ways not previously possible.

The upper classes could, for the first time in any numbers, personally follow their racing fortunes outside Ascot and Newmarket and could also extend their hunting in the shires from weekends to weekdays if they wished. The middle classes used the train to attend their rowing, cricket, football and rugby clubs as they retreated further into the suburbs and they could also participate in a greater number of away fixtures as the railway linked all the playing venues.

Cheap excursion trains allowed the working class to follow their local football and rugby teams (whose fixture lists had grown with the railways) throughout the north of England. Fishing was hugely popular and was catered for with concessionary fares negotiated by angling associations. Warrington Anglers' Association, for example, arranged 750 cheap fares for its members during the 1911 season. All of this was supplemented by 'specials' that took many thousands of people to see:

- professional rowing at Newcastle-upon-Tyne

- cricket at Nottingham, Leeds and Manchester

- rugby at Odsal in Bradford

- bowling at Blackpool

- racing at Chester…

…and many other major and minor venues served by a rail network, which had expanded to over 22,000 miles by 1900.

Playing for fun

Although the element of competition was vital to the professional, it was a matter of relative indifference to the amateur, for whom sport could be classified under Johnson's original dictionary definition of 'that which unbends the mind by turning it from care'.

Notably unathletic, Johnson pronounced that his one experience of hunting had been anything but enjoyable but for many it was the purest recreation of all since the killing of a fox was often the least important consideration. Hunting records show many barren days but they were counted as successes due to the speed of the chases across open country.

Socialising was an important element of hunting and other recreations and much of the language reflects this with many clubs calling themselves 'societies'. The Society of Gentlemen Archers, for example, was established in Darlington in 1758 for the purpose of shooting at targets for a silver medal and to encourage the ancient, noble and manly exercise of archery.

The most famous run in the then history of fox hunting, the Billesdon Coplow hunt of February 24th, 1800, lasted for two and a quarter hours, travelled over twenty-eight miles and failed to kill anything.

There were also days such as that suffered by the North Staffordshire Hounds on November 8th, 1926, when 'there was no scent, no foxes and we all ended up soaking wet'.

The growth of clubs and societies

The Mersey Archery Society (1821) was supported equally by gentlemen and ladies whose shooting partners were drawn by lot. It was also stipulated that no one was allowed to win more than twice in any season.

Although archery was much gentrified during the eighteenth century and most societies were made of the leisured classes, other institutions were less exclusive and at the other end of the social scale fishing societies enjoyed huge popularity.

Walthamstow Fishing and Shooting Society was inaugurated in 1838, with members paying one shilling (5 pence) for a day's fishing on water that extended, from 'France Ware to beyond the coal wharf'. The Derwentwater Anglers Association was established to 'secure the means of recreation to the true sportsman', particularly the working man, 'whose subscription could be paid by a day's labour driving stakes into the stream'.

In Warrington The Jolly Anglers Society was formed in 1848 and any breach of the rather informal rules was penalised by fines levied in drink. This title was not acceptable to the stricter later Victorians who in 1891 changed the name of the club to the Angling Association with formal written rules and fines in hard cash.

Mass participation in fishing developed during the latter half of the nineteenth century and today it is the most popular of all recreational activities based on the number of regular participants. The increase was very noticeable in urban societies such as the one in Sheffield, which grew from 7,000 members in 1860 to 20,000 in 1900. This was largely due to improved cheap rail access to fisheries.

Many early societies were formed by groups of friends seeking diversions. An example of this is the Dresden Boat Club (1839) whose rulebook states that 'any member having once belonged to the club remains as long as the timbers of the boat hold together'. There were many clubs whose purpose was essentially social and this was often apparent in their title:

- The Bullingdon Cricket and Dining Club – established to play cricket once a week but to dine twice a week

- The Billiard Club and News Room of Darlington – whose members had the use of a battered billiard table and five weekly illustrated journals

- The Mutual Improvement Society of Preston – formed by nine friends in 1883 for the purpose of purchasing a billiard table.

Many of the clubs and societies in a particular area had a commonality in their memberships. The previously referred to Mutual Improvement Society of Preston was formed by Richard and Charles Tuson and Joseph Hesketh. All three came from leading local families and established many other clubs in Preston. In Lancaster, Warrington and other areas club records show common membership of bowling, cricket and rowing clubs as well as of literary and philosophical societies.

The titles of some clubs, however, often belied their true nature. The Guildford Rowing Club, established during the 1880s, provided its members with opportunities for family outings of swimming, canoeing and picnic trips. The Warwick Boat Club was so successful as a club for other sports such as tennis, bowls and croquet that rowing ceased altogether and the name alone represented its origins. Early bicycle clubs provided access to the countryside and concentrated on social and recreational activities such as:

- 'the moonlight runs and paper chases' of the Oken Bicycle Club of Warwick (1883)

- the afternoon tea runs to Wilmslow of the Levenshulme Velocipede Club (1869)

- 'very grand ornamental riding around pub yards' – Colchester Bicycle Club (1875)

- the ambitious five day tour of Normandy – the Finsbury Park Cycling Club (1912).

You cannot be serious...

For all such clubs the notion of serious competition was simply inappropriate. This was also the case in the early years of lawn tennis, which was 'a frivolous game for suburban back gardens'.

Even when the All-England Lawn Tennis and Croquet Club initiated its serious championship in 1877, it is recorded that, 'having chosen the best seats for themselves and friends the committee adjourned', an attitude which pervaded the championships for at least ten years or so afterwards.

The priorities of the All-England Club's committee were also apparent in its setting aside of two rest days on the first Friday and Saturday of the tournament in order to avoid a clash with that highlight of the social season, the Eton and Harrow cricket match.

Ironically, that particular match was always fiercely contested, as indeed during the same period and later were the annual Oxford and Cambridge University cricket match and the university boat race.

Such earnest pursuit of victory had certainly not been the intention of Charles Wordsworth, responsible for the inaugural university boat race in 1829. Both events were in fact initially the result of informal arrangements made amongst old school friends. Towards the end of his life Wordsworth criticised the 'professionalism' of the participants, which was far removed from his original concept of 'pure recreation'. By then, however, the desire for sporting excellence had replaced the simple pleasures of participation with the desire for victory.

Recreationalism lives on

Recreationalism flourished throughout the late Victorian and Edwardian periods and into the 1920s and 1930s when, as one commentator put it, recreation changed from 'pleasure pure to pleasure as a restless and rapid escape from work in shops and offices'.

There had been evidence amongst the urban working classes of a restless desire for escape for many years and they took rail excursions to the new seaside resorts in their tens of thousands. They also took up rural pursuits such as fishing and joined cycling and rambling clubs in an effort to break the monotony of their daily lives.

The growing popularity of rambling led to increased demand for access to the privately owned countryside during the 1880s and culminated in the Access to

Mountains Bill (1889). This was overwhelmingly rejected after representations to parliament by the owners of grouse moors.

It was not until 1932 that the mass trespass of Kinder Scout in Derbyshire saw greater access to open land negotiated. This was partly due to the good offices of the Youth Hostel Association and the Ramblers Association at a time when the government was keen to promote 'fitness for service'.

For the members of some sports clubs, physical fitness was more important than their involvement in sport. For many, fitness training became an end in itself and many patented exercise machines came onto the market around the turn of the century.

Perhaps the most bizarre was the 'Rowing Bicycle' which was propelled forwards via a chain linked to a submerged paddle wheel.

These machines represented a move towards non-competitive and largely solitary recreations, such as fishing, rambling and cycling, in which thoughtful reflection replaced combativeness. Although this 'thoughtful reflection' gradually evolved into the 'outward bound' adventurism of the second half of the twentieth century, the early recreationalists were satisfied with the leisurely social gatherings with which they had become so familiar.

There is plenty of evidence of 'leisurely social gatherings' continuing into the twentieth century, e.g.:

- Bolton – where the rugby club failed to find any opponents and nobody seemed to mind (1904)

- Bristol – where the cycling club was quite happy to accept motorcyclists as members (1908)

- Trowbridge – where a club was formed entirely for the purpose of 'recreation' (1913)

- Warrington – where a bowling league was established for the sole purpose of 'cementing good fellowship' (1929)

- Sunningdale – where the Ladies Golf Club changed club days 'to accommodate those who hunt' (1932).

Although organised sport suffered badly during World War II, the truly leisure-orientated pursuits, such as bowling and angling, carried on 'much as usual'. Indeed, the *Mass Observation Archive* mentioned that, unlike World War I, 'a characteristic of this war is that people do play games without a sense of guilt or fear of the white feather' – i.e. being accused of cowardice.

The overriding characteristic of recreationalism had always been its leisurely pace, showing clearly that recreations were activities for gentlemen and ladies only and in which excellence of performance was considered undignified.

Activities such as yachting had developed through aristocratic influence and the sport's fashionable period continued into the eighteenth century with George II as patron of the Cork Yacht Club in 1720 and the Cumberland Fleet becoming the Royal Yacht Club. This connection with the sea was thought to be 'patriotic' as it encouraged marine skills useful to the nation. Similar notions were attached to rowing, which was also highly fashionable in the second half of the eighteenth century.

The gentry established many 'lone boat' clubs such as the Dresden Boat Club in Nottingham, formed in 1839 by Sir William Anstruther and Lord Inverary for an initial membership of seven; six being rowers and one being the steerer. These clubs were popular because they catered for small groups of friends, usually five, seven or nine in number. The Lancaster Rowing Club was formed in 1842 because a group of friends couldn't find eleven for a cricket club.

The various archery societies formed in the eighteenth century as the activity became gentrified had similar aims. One of the oldest was the Toxophilite Society, formed near Manchester in 1780 by Sir Ashton Lever of Alkrington. Archery soon became one of the most fashionable of pastimes, particularly amongst ladies.

Competitive clubs such as the Broughton Archers, which practised near Kersal Moor in Salford, were eventually formed with a membership made up exclusively of wealthy gentlemen. The Staffordshire Bowmen (1791) was patronised by the Earls of Shrewsbury and was an association 'which was the means of so much social intercourse'. The association's shooting grounds were at Alton Towers where, as late as 1870, two hundred archers arrived by special train to shoot and have dinner.

A leisurely game of cricket

The development of cricket was largely dependent on aristocratic patronage, usually in the form of a suitable venue. Local people formed a club at Alcester in 1861 for the purpose of spending summer evenings in 'the pastime of cricket' but found great difficulty in finding a field to play in. Eventually, they petitioned the Marquis of Hertford to 'make available a portion of Ragley Park to enable us to indulge in the healthy pastime of cricket'.

Such philanthropy was also found in the public sector, especially in large urban conurbations where open space was becoming increasingly scarce. In 1846 Lord Morpeth, the Commissioner of Woods and Forests, reserved Victoria Park in Whitechapel for the purpose of cricket since 'the present rage for building was reducing the number of available grounds'. Morpeth also opened Birkenhead Park, the country's first publicly funded park in 1847.

Many parks (both public and private) were named after Victoria either as Queen or Princess. Many 'Victoria Parks' were opened in 1897 to commemorate the monarch's sixtieth year on the throne.

The sports of horse racing, hunting and shooting continued to provide recreation for their leisured supporters, although some questioned the desirability of spending so much time on such frivolous pursuits, which, according to Lord Greville, 'degraded his understanding and made him less respectable in the world'. Evidence of such degradation can be found in his diary and that of Charles Shaw MP, both of which mention shameful behaviour towards the opposite sex.

There were, however, many lighter social diversions like the evening playing at cards, which normally followed a day's shooting, or the Assembly Room dances, which rounded off a day at the races and, of course, the hunt ball was always the social event of the country year. Nicholas Cox in his *Gentlemen's Recreations* (1674) noted that it was common for the hunt to be made up of the local squire and nobility. However, by 1800 hunts began to attract hundreds of followers and by 1860 Anthony Trollope regarded them as a national sport.

By this time many of the newer hunts were supported by a wide social cross section ranging from prosperous tradesmen to the landed gentry: almost anybody who could afford to pay the 'subscription'. Subscription hunts became more widely accessible because of extensions to the railways and were far less exclusive than the ancient hunts like the Quorn, which continued to limit entry to a select few.

Most hunts resembled the Gatewood Fox Hounds of Berwick-on-Tweed with its thirty-seven members, eleven of whom were very minor nobility; or the Norfolk Fox Hounds with twenty-one subscribers paying £500 per year for two days' hunting a week. The Marquis of Cholmondeley helped the Norfolk hunt by encouraging foxes to live on his estate so that members could always be sure of a good day out.

The church and the 'demon drink'

Whilst much recreational activity was sponsored by the gentry, much was also initiated by the church. This is hardly surprising considering the many activities that grew out of 'playing after church' on Sundays.

The local country priest was often involved in hunting, shooting and fishing along with the squire, the doctor and justices of the peace. Archbishop Lang, in his *Sermons* (1913), extolled the virtues of hunting for the clergy, saying that it encouraged some of the finest qualities of human nature: courage, endurance, readiness to face risk comradeship and honourable courtesies.

In the second half of the nineteenth century, clergy were encouraged to become involved in the daily lives of ordinary people – often called 'muscular Christianity' – and they did so in sport, leisure and recreation.

The incidence of church support for sporting clubs is truly astonishing. Of the 120 associations referred to in this book, 86 had priests as officers, committee members, patrons or presidents. Much of the social reform of the Victorian era was motivated by Christian philosophy and was largely implemented by priests, often living in squalid conditions among the working poor. Hence much of the recreational provision for workers began in plans drawn up and promoted by local Christian groups.

In 1845, the Manchester diocese encouraged the major cotton manufacturers to provide a recreation ground, which was used for cricket, quoits and football and where ginger beer and coffee could be bought cheaply. Apart from encouraging healthy exercise, this was a way of keeping people away from public houses at a time when drunkenness was a great social problem.

Also in 1845 the Middlesborough Temperance Society found that four times as many people went to the public house on Sundays as attended church. In 1846 Walsall followed the Manchester initiative and made provision for 'healthy innocent recreation for all classes in cricket, quoits, archery and other games'. Temperance societies generally made a more than significant contribution to the social and recreational welfare of the working poor.

Mechanics Institutes and Working Men's Associations, often with support from local clergy, also played a vital role in providing recreational facilities for the poor.

The Working Men's College in Great Ormond Street, London, organised rambling, rowing and cricket for all on a weekly basis.

John 'Rob Roy' MacGregor, an associate of the above college and an ex-Cambridge University oarsman, was responsible for establishing many 'ragged schools' for London street children. He also popularised canoeing through his trips on rivers in Europe and beyond. Such philanthropy on the part of the church and its representatives was a practical approach to overcoming the twin social evils of delinquency and drunkenness. Virtually any recreational or other acceptable diversion was used in the hope of weaning people away from such pastimes.

The Vale of Derwentwater Angling Association (President, the Reverend Goodfellow) was established to discourage poaching and encourage honest fishing amongst working men. Seven years after its formation the annual report for 1858 claimed that 'instead of a few idle men making dishonest gain we now see numbers of decent working men fishing while poaching has entirely disappeared'.

On the Isle of Wight, the establishment of the Ryde Rowing Club in 1877 (President, the Reverend Mackereth), was deemed to be 'of great benefit for the young men of the town both physically and morally' and in Mansfield in 1874 the local church organised the shop apprentices into the Wanderers Cricket Club.

Many present-day football clubs began life as church teams, including:

- Aston Wesleyan: Aston Villa FC
- Christ Church: Bolton Wanderers FC
- Everton Congregationalist: Everton FC
- St Luke's: Wolverhampton Wanderers FC
- St Mark's: Manchester City FC
- St Mary's, Southampton: Southampton FC
- Trinity Church: Birmingham City FC.

This constructive approach to social problems was endorsed by Barnett's classic text *Towards Social Reform* (1909) in which a close personal knowledge of life amongst the poor was seen as the starting point for any useful provision for those unfortunates whose 'line of leisure was drawn just above sleeping hours and education ended at thirteen years of age'.

Even in the twentieth century church involvement continued in much the same way with clubs such as Sale Harriers being established in 1910 by a group of local churches to stage road races and cross-country runs. Also of major importance was the nationwide development of recreational facilities by YMCAs and YWCAs (Young Men's and Women's Christian Association).

The Sabbath

Any encouragement of recreation by the church met with a strong disapproval of Sunday activity dating back to the condemnation of unlawful sports in the sixteenth century and before. Such disapproval grew in the early nineteenth century as more working people used Sundays for recreation (it being the only day on which they did not have to work). For the relatively leisured church-going middle classes this smacked of unchristian behaviour and several organisations were established to minimise its harmful effects.

The Temperance Movement in 1829, the Lord's Day Observance Society and the Society for the Suppression of Vice in 1831 all lambasted the 'shameful practice of races on Sundays'. It has already been noted that the Lord Mayor of London prohibited the hiring of boats on Sundays in the eighteenth century and the gentrified activity of rowing continued to discriminate against any such activity.

In Nottingham the working-class members of the local rowing club were prevented from using the boats by its middle-class committee. As a result they formed the Nottingham Boat Club in 1894, which positively encouraged Sunday outings.

This was such a momentous occurrence that Arthur Spooner, a club member and talented artist, painted the first ever crew to row on a Sunday and called it 'The First Sunday Outing'. Nearly a century later the painting was found in a back room and sent to auction where it fetched £90,000, which sum secured the financial future of the club.

The new working-class cyclists or 'cads on castors' also presented a problem for Sabbatarians with the Lord's Day Observance Society regularly recording incidences of Sunday cycling. On June 20th, 1904, 1,797 men and 125 women were seen to pass the Red Deer Inn at Croydon en-route to Box Hill, a local beauty spot.

These runs were rarely 'official' outings and some clubs prohibited the wearing of uniforms on Sundays to avoid criticism.

It is perhaps no surprise to find that the gentrified and exclusive game of golf took a 'no play on Sunday' stance. Prior to the inter-war period many clubs copied Warrington Golf Club, which in 1904 'closed the links absolutely on Sundays for both play and promenading'.

The inter-war period saw a more relaxed attitude towards Sunday play and even a stalwart of the Establishment like Arthur Conan Doyle advocated the opening of the Empire Exhibition on Sundays 'so that the poorer people have a chance of seeing the show'.

Such attitudes became far more common following World War II when it became widely felt that events should take place on 'non-working' days such as Saturday afternoons and Sundays, whatever the church might think. In 1944, a long-standing convention was broken when the FA sanctioned Sunday soccer.

As society became progressively more democratic, secularised clubs balloted their members concerning play on Sunday with the majority (such as the Trowbridge Recreation Club in May 1946) receiving the go-ahead providing that 'there would be no tea-making facilities and no bar'.

The trend towards a complete secularisation of society has continued and the last vestige of Sabbatarianism was removed in 1994 when Bills allowing the opening of retail shops and horse racing on Sundays were passed in parliament.

The participation of women

Prior to the eighteenth century it had been unusual to find women involved in sport, except perhaps hawking and horse riding for genteel ladies and feast day activities such as smock racing for peasant women.

However, as increased levels of commercial activity caused breakdowns of the old social order, more prosperous women took small steps towards sporting emancipation.

Such boldness, first seen on the hunting field, did not pass without adverse comment. James Thompson's epic poem 'The Seasons' (1730) criticised the ladies' 'uncomely courage and unbeseeming skill with which the winning softness of their sex is lost'.

A century later, in his *Analysis of the Hunting Field*, Surtees (1830) confirmed their acceptance by acknowledging 'some uncommon performances by women that would put nine-tenths of men to the blush'.

Boating, archery and shooting

The construction of artificial lakes at many country houses encouraged ladies to take up boating away from the public gaze and following the emancipating influence of the Women's Property Act (1870) and the Matrimonial Causes Act

(1878) it was felt, as Lady Greville (1880) said, 'that now everything is changed, it is essential that every English girl should learn to row'.

It had been obvious for some time that women could row, as the crews of fisherwomen competing in the Saltash regatta in Devon had proved. However, it was still widely thought that women could not mature physically if they indulged in strenuous mental or physical activity.

As the women of Devon took up boating, the women of Sussex took up cricket and in the 1780s and 1790s the Bury Common women's team challenged the All-England Eleven (with no response from the men). However, real progress was not made until cricket became a sport in the girls' independent schools.

The general attitude to women was that they made excellent teas but that the cricket pavilion was 'one of the last asylums of the merely male in a changing world', as *The Times* in September 1926 put it.

Despite the above the 1930s saw the establishment of many women's cricket clubs, such as that in Bolton where use of the men's ground was allowed on one day a week and the ladies were generally made to feel like second-class citizens.

Women also made their mark in archery. In 1821 Mersey Archery Society was made up of twenty-nine men and twenty-one women who regularly shot together. The Staffordshire Society, after failing as an all-male club, was very successful as a mixed association in 1863 with Lady Edwards as Patroness and Eleanor Sneyd as President.

Although the ability of women in shooting was equal to that of their male colleagues and their numbers in many societies were greater than men's, the sport never attained truly popular status and remained what *The Times* in 1939 called, 'a primitive, decorative kind of amusement admirable for displaying the female form and productive of social pleasure and friendly rivalry'.

Tennis and golf

Women's sport developed largely in schools and colleges and in the suburban family garden and the private club, where many middle-class women lived in a kind of psychological and physical bondage.

From the 1850s this suburban culture embraced croquet, badminton and later lawn tennis, all of which were designed with women very much in mind. Tennis had evolved from royal tennis via the 'rough and ready' field tennis to the suburban lawn version as a low-skill but convenient social activity.

There was a huge growth of clubs in the last quarter of the nineteenth century, especially in the commuter belt around London. Many had a majority of women members, as in the Dunmow Park club in Essex where in 1896 there were eighteen female and nine male members. The facilities were used almost exclusively by women during the week with special arrangements being made for 'weekday men', and at the Walthamstow club in 1897 there was a rule requiring two courts to be set aside for the sole use of gentlemen on Tuesdays and Thursdays.

Another almost exclusively middle-class sport taken up by women was golf but male golfers were far less inclined than their tennis and archery brothers to allow female access. Women were permitted to play only 'upon such days and subject to such restrictions as the committee from time to time shall determine'. But ... with one million domestic servants giving them more leisure time than their menfolk, it was clear that women would not be denied.

So, whilst female participation was quietly accepted in many clubs, they were denied any executive or voting powers and membership of the larger clubs remained restricted to adult males. Some less central areas saw the establishment of clubs with women as full members and in 1894 the Appleby club in Westmorland had forty-three men and thirty-three women whose subscriptions financed the clubhouse with equal but separate accommodation.

Where golf was very popular it was often impossible for women to integrate as many of the clubs were already fully subscribed with men. At Sunningdale in Berkshire this was partly avoided by the formation in 1906 of a Ladies Club, which negotiated an agreeable rent and affiliation fee with the well-established men's club.

The growth of women's golf and the difficulties it experienced saw the Ladies Golf Union formed in 1893. This helped to improve playing conditions and organised a Ladies' Championship at Lytham and St Anne's that same year. Considering their popularity amongst socially well-connected women, it is not surprising that tennis and golf gave women their first opportunity to compete in the Olympic Games. They were thought to be essentially ladylike activities, not too strenuous and could be easily accomplished fully clothed.

The 'rational dress' debate

The prudery surrounding women's sport gave rise to strict regulations about appropriate dress, which must have made certain activities extremely difficult.

The Oxford University Women's Boat Club stipulated in 1906 that 'girls shall have a draw string in their skirts so that no ankle is exposed'. Despite this, the Skiff Racing

Association still complained in March 1907 that 'the costumes worn by the ladies were unnecessarily scanty'.

In 1898, the Kendal Women's Hockey Club rules stated that 'skirts must be no more than six inches above the ground all round' to be accompanied by a green blouse, white collar, white tie and green beret.

In 1914, Councillor Margaret Ashton of Manchester Corporation thought that 'men were allowed to witness women's swimming competitions in a manner quite indecent'.

Even as late as 1936 the Alpha Ladies Rowing Club were advised to clad themselves 'in long blue stockings, black shorts, tops covering the arm-pits and berets to cover long hair'.

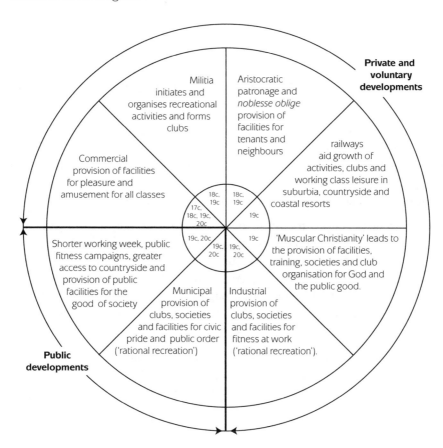

FIGURE 5.1 Main influences on recreational development through the centuries

Such prudery, however, was not universal and in 1914 it was debated in Manchester whether or not to allow mixed bathing. Inquiries were made of other towns with eighteen replies being favourable and twenty-six not. *All* the favourable replies came from London boroughs and since Manchester feared falling behind the capital it was decided to let men and women swim together for the first time.

Swimming clubs had long had ladies' sections meeting separately from men's and sometimes (as in Stockport) in baths built specially for them. Ladies' swimming galas were held in Netherfield, Stockport, Tyldesley and Warrington throughout the 1870s and effectively boosted memberships with the Netherfield club having fifty-five men and fifty-three women members in 1890 with similar parity in most of the Manchester clubs. Nottingham Ladies Swimming Club was established in 1905 and in 1914 the Park Swimming Club in Tottenham had seventy-seven men and seventy-seven women fully subscribed.

Whilst mixing of the sexes in swimming did not really occur until World War I, it was rather more immediate in cycling and was extremely important because it allowed all women an access to physical recreation that had previously been the preserve of the leisured classes. By 1890 membership of the CTC was 60,000 with over 20,000 women.

Women were important members of clubs everywhere, providing, for example, five of the nine Cyclists Touring Club committee members in Bristol in 1912 and organising all of the Darlington Cycling Club's summer runs in 1914. The holding of responsible positions by women increased during and after World War I due to the absence of many men and the fact that many of them failed to return.

Despite strenuous efforts to encourage more women to participate, it was only in the leisured classes that any real progress was made. Athletics was one of the few sports to attract other classes and the Women's Amateur Athletic Association was formed in 1922 with support largely from lower-middle- and working-class girls. These girls also took part in cycling and hiking, positively encouraged by the Youth Hostel Association (otherwise known as 'Your Husband Assured'), which was formed in 1930.

However, the vast majority of working-class women simply refrained from any sport and were far more likely to be found 'going to the cinema, dancing, drinking and promenading', as the *Mass Observation Archive* noted in 1942.

It is not surprising that working women chose a passive role in recreation for they not only worked hard but were also aware of the cultural barrier that separated them from activities largely carried out in private members' clubs.

Many of the activities under discussion in this chapter provided the 'well-to-do' with further opportunities to confirm their superior social status by demonstrating a leisurely lifestyle. This was calculated to consolidate their position as gentlemen and this in turn was reaffirmed by the amateur ethic and institutionalised in the sporting club. It is to the evolution of both of these that we shall turn in the following chapter.

QUESTIONS

RECREATIONALISM

1   Why was it that provision for recreation became nationally important in the early years of the twentieth century?

2   Why and by whom was it considered less than acceptable to take sport seriously?

3   How did the temperance movement utilise sport in its fight against alcohol?

4   Why were many sports considered unsuitable for women?

5   Account for the importance of tennis and cycling as activities for women.

6   What was 'rational dress' and what were the issues it provoked?

Suggested further reading

Bailey, P., *Leisure and Class in Victorian England* (Routledge, 1978)
Fulford, R. (ed.), *The Greville Memoirs* (Batsford, 1963)
Hargreaves, J., *Sport, Power and Culture* (Polity Press, 1986)

chapter six

AMATEURISM

No manner of artificer or craftsman be allowed to play on pain of 20 shillings fine … every nobleman and other landowners might play without penalty.

(Concerning Unlawful Sports Act, 1541)

To allow a mixing of professional and amateur is as senseless and impractical as the negro fraternising with the refined and cultured members of the civilised world.

(Whitney, 1894, p. 11)

Amateurism ('amo' meaning 'I love') was derived from an eighteenth-century appreciation of the fine and polite arts by gentlefolk who dabbled in activities without any desire for excellence. This explained their dislike of people who did try hard to be very good. Such people were professionals and others referred to as 'quasi-amateurs' or 'pseudo professionals'.

Gentlemen took part in activities 'for the love of it' whilst the others took things far too seriously and were therefore disqualified from being gentlemen. Anthony Trollope, the Victorian novelist, explains this perfectly in his book, *British Sports and Pastimes*, published in 1868.

Trollope commented that: 'playing billiards is the amusement of a gentleman but to play billiards eminently well is the life's work of a man who in learning to do so can hardly have continued to be a "gentleman" in the best sense'.

The prejudice against excellence of performance was underpinned by a similar distaste for trade learned in classical education, which stressed the Athenian concept of a class of people born to rule.

The Victorians developed this concept into almost a religion and praised the benefits of a strict and unchanging social hierarchy. This produced an amateur ethic which preached the exclusion of the professional at any cost: which was made easier by the peculiarly feudal nature of English society.

A society divided

The division of class based on the ownership of land had constituted English society for centuries until the rise of mercantilism threatened to undermine it in the eighteenth century. Despite huge social, political and economic inequalities the ruling class in Georgian Britain remained both entrenched and immune from revolutionary trends. This is explained by:

■ the deferential nature of the English character

■ flexibility of the ruling class

■ the prospect of social mobility through industrialisation.

The ruling classes consolidated their position by taking over the great public schools to the extent that between 1700 and 1780 the percentage of noblemen's sons at Eton, Harrow, Winchester or Westminster rose from 17 to 72 per cent.

By 1807, the peerage controlled the election of one-third of members of parliament with other sons taking up other top jobs through patronage and purchase. There was a daily round of social amusements which supplanted the traditional gentlemen's pursuits of dinners, play-houses, cards and gambling and they were the first to make involvement in sport a gentlemanly activity. In doing so they appropriated activities such as bowling and rowing from their social inferiors, including:

■ bowling at the New Exchange coffee house in 1784

■ boating from the Star and Robin Hood coffee houses in the 1790s

■ the Monarch Boat Club at Eton College in 1793

■ the Isis Boat Club at Westminster School in 1790

■ the White Conduit Cricket Club formed by 'Westminsters' in 1782.

Appropriation and gentrification

This appropriation and gentrification of 'common' sports led to rules and regulations (where any existed) being refined to meet the supposed higher moral standards of gentlemen players.

As bowling became fashionable at coffee houses, 'Rules and Instructions for the Art of Bowling' was published in 1786 by a Society of Gentlemen, seeking 'to remove doubts and prevent disputes'.

Rugeley Bowling Green's 'New Rules and Orders to be Observed' (1776) contained 45 laws, including sanctions against betting, blaspheming or any activity 'likely to be unsuitable for civil company'.

The boat clubs of the Star and Robin Hood coffee houses rowed against other similar one-boat clubs on the Chelsea stretch of the River Thames in 'straight away' racing which valued scientific oarsmanship over the 'fixing and fouling' that was common in those times.

In cricket the genteel concept of fair play took precedence over winning, with the Hambledon Club's minutes of May 1774 noting 'that every cricket player that gets thirty runs shall be obliged to give up his batt for the innings'.

As the eighteenth century wore on and the number of public school graduates increased, the greater became the desire to exclude socially unacceptable elements from the field of play.

There was much disapproval of gentlemen playing with those 'not compatible with their rank and station' but this has to be set against the background of the French Revolution which had made the English aristocracy extremely nervous.

The Times of September 2nd, 1790 (only months after the French Revolution) noted that 'the state, by cricket rules, discriminates the Great and on either side the great game is played': making the point that rules and order are as necessary in the game of life as they are in sports.

In rowing, professionals were ousted by gentlemen who wouldn't cheat and in horse racing the Newmarket stewards began their campaign to dominate the sport by winning the legal right to 'warn off' undesirables from Newmarket Heath, even though it was open public land.

Despite the inclination to exclude unsuitable persons from their sporting activities, the gentlemen maintained a social responsibility in supporting the sporting endeavours of their social inferiors. One aspect of this was gambling on the 'wrangles' or contests of tradesmen, which were justified as 'finding employment for the labouring mechanic'.

This was an urban equivalent of the old feudal obligation of aristocratic landowners to support tenants in times of need and which also included sponsorship of local sporting events. It is however clear that these age-old customs were adopted by the new class of public school-educated gentlemen to develop their own social exclusivity rather than social responsibility.

Equality versus social control

Although the desire to keep the lower orders at arm's length was partly sheer snobbery, it was also seen as necessary social control at a time of revolution and unrest at home and abroad. A breakdown of the class structure was seen as a precursor of anarchy and many thought that the extension of the electoral franchise following the Napoleonic Wars (granted in 1832) was the beginning of the end for civilisation as they knew it: even though the vote remained in the hands of the wealthier classes.

A letter in *The Times* of April 13th, 1840 signed by forty clergymen expressed the fears of many in noting 'the fearful progress of socialism, a system which tramples all decency underfoot and sets lawful authority at defiance, bringing bloodshed, anarchy and ruin'.

Set against this background, the 'amateurs' must have seen their fight as a struggle for a civilisation based on heredity, rank and nobility, and Christian privilege, against those who 'honoured no one except for his own merit and his own deeds'.

This thought was well expressed by the warden of Radley College in 1849 when he said that 'a gentleman both knows and is thankful that God instead of making all men equal has in fact made them all most unequal'. It was this unequalness that the gentleman amateur sought to maintain.

The position of the gentleman amateur was soon threatened by further social reform:

■ the Ten Hours Act of 1847 gave workers time off on Saturdays

■ the Reform Acts of 1867 and 1884 gave the vote to various classes of working men

■ the Labour Representation Act of 1869 promoted the idea of working-class members of parliament

- the Education Act of 1870 extended education to the poorest working-class children

- the Union Chargeability Act of 1876 enabled workers to move around more easily.

In 1888, Mrs Beeton made the telling remark that events were daily 'removing the landmarks between the mistress and her maid, the master and his man'. It was precisely these landmarks that the gentleman amateur was determined to maintain in his sporting life, even if he couldn't do so elsewhere.

The initial battle was not with the full-time professional who emerged later in the nineteenth century, but with the quasi-amateur who, irrespective of whether he had taken payment for his sporting activities, was definitely regarded as socially inferior.

The perceived link between popular recreations and civil disturbance was seen as a threat to the status quo and reached back through the centuries to the times of prohibited and unlawful sports.

Working people took full advantage of the long-established holiday sports, which together with the ever-present alcohol resulted in good-natured but excessively boisterous behaviour. However, in the context of the social unrest that continued long after the battle of Waterloo, the authorities banned many sports as possible sources of civil disobedience or even revolution.

In 1819 an example of this occurred at Berkhamstead Common, where sports had been held from 'time out of mind'; but in this particular year Lord Berkamstead directed that people should be told not to come or else be prosecuted. The local constable asked why to be told that his Lordship feared a mass trespass by 'idle people'. Eventually, the 'criketting' was allowed to take place but the ban on 'women bruising for a prize, trap-ball, quoits and Dandy horses' remained, along with a refusal to extend licensing hours.

During this post-war era it did not take much for the new class of gentlemen to imagine a sporting revolution including working people at rural sports and tradesmen at organised sports. It was this historical precedent which provided a claimed Christian and patriotic justification for actions which in fact were motivated by social and cultural reasons.

This is shown very well in the attitude of the Warrington Regatta secretary in 1844 when he complained that 'the public notice of rural sports with my name on it (erroneously) will militate against the good opinion of regatta subscribers who heartily disapprove of them'. Rowing was particularly rigorous in enforcing a social apartheid.

The application of personal animosity towards members of the despised class of quasi-amateur in the form of the crew of 'The Wave' was evident at Lancaster Regatta in 1844. Having been accused of fouling, this crew of 'mechanics' were refused the prize of their event, to which their captain took considerable exception. He explained in a letter to the regatta committee that,

> **I am compared to you but a humble individual, but there was great dissatisfaction that the prize for amateurs was twenty guineas whilst that for the poorer class was but £3; showing anything but a liberal spirit towards those in a lower sphere of life.**

No reply was forthcoming but the minutes of the regatta for September 30th of that year contain the committee's response:

> **No notice whatever was taken of this most despicable attempt to discredit the regatta, which has been conducted in every respect to the satisfaction of all.**

Henley Regatta, the rowing world's leading event, managed to maintain its gentlemanly character by distancing itself from taverns or public houses, whilst the leading club, London Rowing Club, secured its social purity by making a strict division between gentlemen amateurs and tradesmen amateurs and by ensuring that 'the barriers between them were not broken down'.

In cricket, the tone of the game had been set by gentlemen since the early eighteenth century, so that by 1853 *The Times* was able to praise the past season as played more closely in the true spirit upon which the health of the game depended, knowing that this had been achieved by the imposition from above of an etiquette and hierarchy consistent with the contemporary social prejudices. This had not been achieved without some undesirable elements being excluded from participation and even, on occasion, spectating. The latter was made that much easier with the advent of enclosed cricket grounds.

In 1858 hordes of Newcastle working men were denied access to the cricket ground on the pretext that they were 'not respectable'. It is significant that of all sports, it was cricket that last dropped the distinction between 'players' and 'gentlemen' in 1963.

The *Saturday Review* of April 20th, 1867 stated the view of the gentlemen amateur very clearly: 'The facts of his being civil and never having competed for money are NOT sufficient to make a man a gentleman as well as an amateur'; and, as we have seen, gentlemen amateurs could and did compete for money without losing their amateur status.

The argument sometimes used to explain the exclusion of the quasi-amateur, the semi-professional and the professional was his higher level of expertise, which made competing against him unfair. And yet, at the same time, many amateurs boasted of beating professionals in horse races, 'Gentlemen against Players' cricket matches and in various practice matches at rowing.

The inescapable conclusion is that social prejudice alone explained the Victorian attitude towards the working man and all his activities.

It is therefore ironic that his very exclusion simply encouraged the growth of alternative forms of sport, which further threatened the amateur ethic.

The truly amateur tradesman, seeing his social superiors winning substantial prize money, became even more inclined to supplement his wages with sporting earnings. This combined with a growing and increasingly competitive leisure market, eventually produced full-time professionals and the thorough professionalisation of sport.

Gate money and 'broken time'

Sport's amateur governing bodies often quoted 'the curse of gate money, which enabled the man of lower rank to earn large salaries' when criticising the spread of professionalism. They also condemned spectatorism as undermining the true nature of sport. The trend towards paying to watch sport, particularly cricket, football and rugby, was generating large sums to pay players' wages and this encouraged even more working men to contemplate sport as an occupation.

The first demands were for 'broken time' payments for time lost at work when playing sport. This was seen as 'paying wages' and vigorously opposed by the amateur sports bodies. Such payments had been made in cricket since the mid-nineteenth century and were formally sanctioned as wages in association football in 1885. They first appeared in rugby during the 1870s when local derbies in the north of England were attracting crowds of 6,000 but international matches in London were only drawing 4,000.

In the north the men who played were miners, mill hands, foundry workers and tradesmen who earned around twenty-five shillings (£1.25) for a five and a half day week and could ill afford to lose half a day's pay to play football. Sports such as rowing, tennis and golf found it relatively easy to marginalise those of the artisan class since both financial and social limitations excluded them at club level. In football and cricket they were largely incorporated at appropriately lower levels.

In rugby, however, whose overwhelming popularity lay in the north, it proved impossible for the gentlemen in London to impose their will. The Rugby Football Union (RFU) disapproved of nationwide cup or league competitions but allowed various county committees freedom to control their own local affairs with the result that the Yorkshire committee established the Yorkshire Challenge Cup.

This became an obsession and set a northern precedent, encouraging fierce competition, huge crowds and substantial payments to players for expenses and broken time. It also led to stringent rules on the transfer of players (1888), which were strictly enforced by the Rev. Frank Marshall, headmaster of Almondbury Grammar School, Huddersfield. In 1893 an RFU bye-law stressed the amateur nature of the game and confirmed that its headquarters were in London, 'where all general meetings shall be held'.

Representatives of several northern clubs placed a motion at such a meeting on September 20th, 1893, asking that 'players be allowed compensation for bona fide loss of time'. This was rebuffed with the reply that 'the above principle is contrary to the true interest of the game and its spirit'.

Two years later, in 1895, the RFU passed even more anti-professional regulations, which led to the now famous meeting of northern clubs at Huddersfield's George Hotel at which a 'Northern Union' was established.

This new organisation 'repudiated any idea of professionalism and was determined to punish any departure from this principle', whilst concurrently making such departures inevitable by starting a northern league and two further cup competitions.

It was such behaviour that led amateur gentlemen to conclude that there was 'an inclination to kick over the traces in the provinces where some very crude notions of amateurism and sport still prevail, particularly in athletics, cycling and football'. Such conclusions saw them redouble their efforts to retain overall control of sport even though the tide of events was rapidly engulfing them.

Initially, the Northern Union took great pains to exclude the true professional from its activities and its records demonstrate just how conscientious it was in this respect. For example, the minutes of November 3rd, 1899 mention: '66 special permits to play in tomorrow's matches, some being conditional on the men working on Friday and Saturday'.

Despite these efforts, however, the sheer scale of the task was beyond the Union's administrative capacity so that by 1900 the regular weekly issue of permits to play was discontinued and replaced by the occasional prosecution of particularly blatant examples of professionalism. This included instances of unemployed men playing for money, which was obviously not compensation for wages lost by being away from work in order to play rugby.

International decline

As far as the governing bodies were concerned this 'kicking over the traces' was damaging the nature and spirit of sport and was seen as being responsible for the decline in British sporting fortunes. This was first remarked upon in cricket when the English team lost to the Australians in 1882 – a horrifying defeat which was notified in the obituary columns of the *Sporting Times* of September 6th. The sentiment was echoed in *The Times* of July 6th, 1914 when Leander Rowing Club lost to Harvard University at the Henley Royal Regatta with a commemoration of British rowing 'which passed away at Henley on July 4th'.

This decline is also noted in athletics, cycling, football, rugby and even bowling, where 'a certain slackness in the spirit of our clubs' was recognised. This was attributed to 'the accursed greed for gold' which reduced the amounts of truly amateur talent while strengthening foreign opposition, which was itself contaminated by professional behaviour.

One of Baron de Coubertin's prime motives in his promotion of a renewed Olympic Games was to support the amateur ideal and combat the rise of professionalism. Unfortunately, as we now know, it was to have exactly the opposite effect.

Disappointing British results at the Games of 1908 and 1912 led to more worries about the growth of play on Sundays and fuelled concerns that sport had gone too far in pursuit of excellence, which reflected a horrible decadence in English society.

This left governing bodies of sport with the choice of taking up the foreign challenge by adopting less than amateur methods or withdrawing from international events and satisfying themselves with domestic competition in which gentlemen could meet gentlemen on level terms.

The FA looked back with evident pride to the first seven cup finals, which had been contested by only four clubs, each with an unmistakable social background:

- The Royal Engineers (officers and gentlemen)
- Old Etonians (ex-public school)

81

- Oxford University (ex-public school)
- The Wanderers (ex-public school).

World War I intervened before any resolution of this dilemma had been reached but the war itself helped to harden attitudes against the reduction of the true sporting spirit which was seen as instrumental in the victory over an evil and unsportsmanlike enemy.

Difficult though it is to believe today, there was an element of English society – usually public school-educated officers and gentlemen – that regarded the war as 'a sportsmen's game to be played with our enemies'. It was not uncommon for such officers to lead charges against the enemy by punting a soccer or rugby ball towards the machine guns. One such individual, the international rugby player E.R. Mobbs DSO, who died in 1917 at the battle of Passchendale, is commemorated annually in the Mobbs Memorial Match between the East Midlands and the Barbarians.

However, further depressing results at post-war Olympic Games resulted in a loosening of amateur principles; not only in the professionalisation of training methods but also the acceptance that payment of certain expenses was justified in the pursuit of the best possible performances. So, in 1929 for example, the British Olympic Association allowed broken time payments to be paid to members of the national football team for the first time.

Immediately following World War I there was a temporary return to pure amateurism in domestic competition because slow demobilisation procedures delayed the return of professional sportsmen. However, the inexorable professionalisation of sport continued with renewed vigour during the depression of the 1920s and 1930s and set against this trend it is not surprising that there was also a resurgence of nineteenth century amateur exclusivity.

The exclusion of 'undesirables'

As we have seen, the exclusion of undesirables was often physical. At the Fulwood Race Course in Preston in 1805 a resolution was passed 'to keep the course shares from passing into the hands of those not approved by the members' so that 'none but noblemen and gentlemen should be admitted to the enclosure'.

In the same year, the minutes recorded that undesirables were ejected from the newly erected grandstand for 'foul language and improper behaviour'. Apparently, even a Mrs Brierley and her guests were subject to ejection as a result of some unspeakable activity. Similarly in Darlington, it was relatively easy to exclude those who were unsuitable for genteel company from the enclosed shooting compound of the local society of archers: as on July 8th, 1797, when a Mr Hodgson was expelled for 'having made use of very improper language and abused and ill-treated all the gentlemen present without an apology'.

Such physical exclusions were easier if grounds were enclosed, so that the authorities in cricket, racing, early archery, bowling and even rowing were able to monitor both spectators and participants in order to maintain the tone and style of play to their satisfaction. There were, of course, other, rather more subtle means of exclusion utilised by these and other sports.

Certain forms of language and behaviour were considered compulsory for members, as were very particular styles of dress and subscription levels, which excluded all but the more prosperous from membership.

Membership cards became vital 'in order to prevent all objectionable persons entering under the plea of belonging to the club'. Some clubs, like the Dresden Boat Club whose membership 'shall not exceed six on any consideration whatever', simply confined membership to word of mouth recommendation.

Blackballing

All gentlemen's clubs operated a 'black ball' system when electing new members. Each member had one white ball and one black ball. These were placed in a bag to register their approval (white ball) or disapproval (black ball) of a potential new member when his name came up for consideration. Eighty-nine out of the 125 clubs referred to in this book used this method, the strictest being the Moseley United Quoit and Bowling Club, which stipulated that 'one black ball should exclude'. This meant that if even one member had placed a black ball in the bag the person under consideration would be excluded from membership.

Most clubs satisfied themselves with a proportion of one black ball in three whilst the most democratic was the Darlington Billiard Club (1863) whose new members were simply elected by a straight majority of existing members present. Of course, the most exclusive clubs and associations such as the Jockey Club, the MCC and Henley Royal Regatta refrained from any election and organised membership by invitation and appointment only.

Admiring this last approach, Baron de Coubertin recreated it in the procedure of the International Olympic Committee, which remains in force today. Similarly, the Amateur Rowing Association constitution provides for the non-elective appointment of representatives from Cambridge and Oxford Universities, the Leander Club, the London Rowing Club and the Thames Rowing Club, all of which reflects the priority and precedence given to gentlemen in the original constitutions of the first clubs.

Application for membership usually entailed filling out a form, requiring the provision of several personal references, banking details and, particularly in the latter part of the nineteenth century, one's occupation or profession. At that time there were many prosperous tradesmen seeking membership of gentlemen's clubs whose members would wish to exclude them on social and cultural grounds. This often caused considerable ill feeling amongst some members and many minute books note that perfectly decent people had been excluded on the whim of a very small number of members.

Such exclusions could have surprising consequences: the Lord Mayor of Chester, having been excluded on social grounds as a boy from the Chester Regatta, took considerable satisfaction in declining the Presidency of the event in 1934 with the national press headlining the story as 'Snobbery in the Rowing World'.

Much mid-Victorian exclusivity derived from the public school culture which affected most amateur sport, initially in the south of England but later elsewhere, and was thus notably strong in those areas which fed such schools.

One such area was London's Blackheath, described in the 1870s as a glorious place with roads fragrant with lime blossom and gardens full of trees and shrubs.

It is not surprising that the Blackheath area produced some of the earliest cricket, hockey, football, rugby and running clubs, all of which were established by boys returning from public schools. It was in areas such as this that the public school code of amateurism was merged with affluent suburban recreation to form an alliance of wealth and social status, which filled sport with a new idealism.

This idealism saw the lower classes segregated from the social élite – even when they were participating in the same forms of exercise.

This same amateur idealism prompted the establishment of the Football Association in 1863, at a meeting of London-based public school old boys' clubs to agree on terms of competition whilst also trying to restrict participation to their own social class.

Even rock-climbing – today regarded as the most open of sporting activities – began in a similar way in 1857 when the Alpine Club was formed by Leslie Stephen, an Oxford University professor. This caused mountaineering to become fashionable very quickly but it continued to exclude tradespersons until well into the twentieth century. The most famous such exclusion was that of Alfred Mummery who was 'blackballed' in 1880 by the Alpine Club because his father was a tradesman. His well-publicised response to this snub was his famous ascent of the dangerous Mount Grepon in the French Alps.

Amateurism and those 'darned mechanics'

Whilst it was relatively easy to exclude 'undesirables' at club level it was almost impossible to do so where tradesmen amateurs could not be fairly excluded from open competition with gentlemen amateurs. Sports governing bodies sought to overcome this difficulty by continually redefining amateurism in increasingly more exclusive terms. By the 1870s the Amateur Athletic Association had finally decided that an amateur was any person who had never:

- competed in any open competition
- competed for public money
- competed for admission money
- taught athletic exercises as a livelihood
- competed with a professional for a prize.

Other governing bodies adopted the above definition as a basis for their own policies of exclusion and *The Times* spoke for them all in a leading article of April 26th, 1880, when it proclaimed that: '… the outsiders, artisans, mechanics and suchlike troublesome persons can have no place found for them. To keep them out is a thing desirable on every count and so no base mechanic arms need be suffered to thrust themselves in here'.

Guilt by association was a dominant theme so that any player competing with a quasi-amateur or professional would himself become contaminated. Even the acceptance of genuine expenses was sufficient to exclude players from strictly amateur events.

Americans were particularly likely to be guilty of this and both their lacrosse team in 1885 and the Vesper Boat Club from Philadelphia in 1905 were banned from competition in England for 100 years for receiving commercially raised funds for their travelling expenses.

Both exclusion orders were rescinded when English governing bodies began to allow expenses within their own organisations during the 1920s and 1930s. In modern times it is commonplace to provide such expenses to foreign competitors in order to encourage their participation. A good example is the £5,000 provided by the stewards of Henley Regatta to the Russian international squad so that they could attend the event in 1987.

These rigorous definitions of amateurism allowed event organisers to create several categories of competitor, thus allowing the gentleman amateur to refrain from open competition when he thought it appropriate. This affected every form of sporting competition, even rural sports like those at Linton in Cambridgeshire, where in 1891 the events were segregated into those for:

- tradesmen
- cottagers
- labourers
- labouring boys
- amateurs.

Amateur purity and 'suitable occupations'

There was a heightened awareness of social acceptability at club level so that, for instance, the new Blackheath Harriers in 1868 stipulated that gentlemen only should be members. Such clubs were often full of members of other similar clubs so that the Blackheath club provided winter training facilities for several local rowing clubs and even allowed one of its committee to become the first secretary of the Amateur Athletic Association in 1880.

Clubs even changed their names to indicate their distancing themselves from socially questionable activities, so we find the Eccentric Bicycle Club renamed as the Walthamstow Bicycle Club in 1878 and the Jolly Anglers becoming the Warrington Angling Association in 1891.

Many clubs added the word 'Amateur' to their titles during the 1870s and 1880s in order to underline their status, and many golf clubs inserted 'the etiquette of golf as laid down by the Royal and Ancient Golf Club has been adopted as a bye-law of this club' into their rules in order to reassure potential members of the club's social credentials.

Some clubs even specified suitable occupations for members. This wasn't strictly necessary as membership was usually expensive enough to exclude 'the wrong sort of chap'. Beccles Golf Club in Suffolk suggested that, in addition to gentlemen with private means, suitable members would be:

- naval officers
- military officers
- clergymen
- masters of endowed schools.

However, playing fees of thirty shillings (a working man's weekly wage in 1899) were sufficient to exclude the artisans, mechanics and suchlike 'troublesome persons' referred to by *The Times* twenty years earlier.

Sailing clubs found themselves in an awkward position in following the age-old tradition of allowing professionals to take the helm or steer in races. This became increasingly unacceptable and was positively frowned upon when the Amateur Rowing Association banned people who worked 'in or about boats' in 1883.

In 1886 the Warrington Sailing Club had a membership of 'amateurs only' and Rule 2 excluded all help from watermen – defined as 'persons who had at any time earned their living on trading vessels'.

The Fambridge Sailing Club in Essex modified this slightly and required that 'yachts must be steered by members of the club and no paid hand in any race shall touch the tiller after the starting gun'.

Sailing clubs were particularly hierarchical since they were based upon the naval pattern of command; and so Fambridge SC had categories for:

- Commodore
- Vice-Commodore
- Captain
- Lieutenant
- Private member.

It also had distinctive uniforms and badges for the club's officers.

No sport was exempt from rigorous self-appraisal in the pursuit of amateur purity and even the small provincial clubs generally followed the line laid down by their governing body in London; so that:

- 1877: the Tyldesley Swimming Club in Lancashire followed the Metropolitan Swimming Clubs Association in disqualifying 'those termed professional'

- 1878: the Cestreham Bicycle Club in Buckinghamshire immediately adopted the rules of the new National Cycling Union

- 1903: the Warrington Bowling League followed the English Bowling Union by blacklisting 21 players.

Factions and fighting

The exclusion of the quasi-amateur from sport organised by the London-based governing bodies had the effect of creating several factions in the domestic sporting scene. These were based on the distinction between those who worked for a living with their hands (quasi-amateurs) and those who did not (amateurs) and led in turn to the establishment of separate governing bodies for working men's sports:

- the Yorkshire and Lancashire cricket leagues during the 1870s

- the Northern Cross Country Association in 1882

- the Northern Counties Amateur Swimming Association in 1889

- the National Amateur Rowing Association in 1890

- the Northern Counties Athletic Association in 1895

- the Rugby League in 1922.

The sentiments expressed by the founders of the Northern Counties Athletic Association reflected a general feeling in proclaiming that 'they could very well do without the South and hoped that the Northern members will treat the Southerners with contempt'.

The north–south sporting split reflected a social, cultural and economic apartheid that was apparent elsewhere in society in living standards, political affiliations and daily custom and which became ever more obvious between the turn of the century and the 1920s. *The Times* referred to the General Strike of 1926 in November of that year as a symptom of the 'post-war class cleavage from which the country suffered'.

The exclusion of working people from full participation in organised sport was simply a reflection of their routine exclusion from the social and economic benefits enjoyed by others.

It was hoped that some democratisation might have followed a debate on the relaxation of the amateur rule in sport held in the Commons on April 7th, 1937, when the rule was defined as: 'a man who earns his living by his hands is not eligible as an amateur'.

The general feeling in the House was that this was indeed acceptable – not surprising considering the educational, social, financial and political affiliations of the Honourable Members present at the debate. However, there were, according to the reports, 'many Honourable Members in all parts of the House, who would like to see the amateur rule revised'. Sadly, this had to wait until the arrival of the post-war Labour government in 1945.

Despite the 'class cleavage' and the cultural and geographical divisions, there were bastions of support for the gentleman amateur in the provinces and these were usually centred on particular clubs, which were run by the 'right class of person'. For example:

- Manchester Cricket Club
- Royal Chester Rowing Club
- Northern Lawn Tennis Club
- Gosforth Rugby Union Club
- Warrington Swimming Club
- Lytham and St Anne's Golf Club.

These organisations administered sport in their areas with a strictness that pleased the governing bodies in London and they were often rewarded with prestigious events such as international trials for rowing on the River Dee in Chester and the Northern Lawn Tennis Championships in Didsbury, Manchester, which were modelled on Olympic rowing trials and Wimbledon respectively.

Such events only served to expose the difficulties common to much grass-roots sport which resulted from unsympathetic control from London. Many sports complained of harsh amateur rulings, pointing out that this simply caused support for their events 'to leech away to more popular branches of athletics'.

This division of organisation at national and regional levels led to poor communications and resulted in contradictory situations in which amateurs appeared to act like professionals and vice versa:

- Quasi-amateur rugby union players in the north were banned from Amateur Athletic Association events and yet Alfred Tysoe of Salford Harriers, also a quasi-amateur, was selected to represent Britain at the 1900 Olympic Games. (He won.)

- Northern Rugby Union players who received expenses and broken time were told that they could not be paid at all for playing during World War I.

- The Northern Rugby Union, having sanctioned 'pay for play', decided not to accept a man suspended as a quasi-amateur by the RFU in case it jeopardised its own amateur status.

- The Football Association refused to reinstate a professional player, as an amateur, even though he had played county cricket as an amateur for years.

Numerous other such contradictions only served to bring the management of sport into disrepute in the eyes of a general public that was increasingly interested in watching the best possible sporting performances regardless of the status of the players.

Such confusion assumed international proportions when European sport (always regarded as quasi-amateur by English governing bodies) created international governing bodies to regulate international competitions. Consequently, the FA refused to join the Fédération Internationale de Football Association (FIFA) in 1904 until its regulations were brought more into line with English customs. At the same time the Amateur Football Association was established in 1908 by clubs who were offended by the level of professionalism allowed by the FA.

Similarly, the Amateur Rowing Aassociation (ARA) refused to join the Fédération Internationale Sociétés d'Aviron (FISA), which had been formed in 1892, because it regarded English amateur status as superior to that of foreign associations, which allowed tradesmen to compete with gentlemen. This caused the ARA acute embarrassment when, preparing the Olympic regatta of 1948, it found that membership of FISA was an absolute requirement of the IOC.

Preparation for the Olympics of 1908 had required the establishment of the British Olympic Committee in 1906. The main motivator here was the Baron Desborough, who was also President of the MCC, the Lawn Tennis Association (LTA) and the Amateur Associations of athletics, fencing and wrestling as well as a steward of the Henley Royal Regatta. So, it rather goes without saying that the new Olympic Committee applied the amateur rule universally and rigorously despite poor Olympic performances in 1896 and 1900 from the gentlemen amateurs.

In Athens in 1896 there had been barely 100 competitors, with the English taking a purely recreational part in cycling, fencing, shooting, rowing, swimming, gymnastics, tennis and athletics.

Typical of the English approach was the participation of the men's doubles team in the tennis tournament. This occurred only because some English players who happened to be at the Games anyway found that the only way they could secure a court to play on was to officially enter the Games. All the available courts had been block booked by the Games Committee.

There were no official British teams at either the 1900 or 1904 Games, so when the 1908 games were awarded to London it became a matter of national prestige to produce an effective and united response.

However, the first experiences of the new British Olympic Committee were not encouraging. No government financial help was available so a Franco-British exhibition was arranged to raise funds to build the Olympic stadium (the White City Stadium) at Shepherds Bush.

The government made no grants for the entertainment of foreign athletes although, according to *The Times* of July 7th, 1908, it 'had always been in favour of putting international hospitality on an organised basis'. These Games were the last at which the host country had full jurisdiction over the sports as there were so many protests concerning administration and the decisions of the (British) judges. The atmosphere was badly affected by the antagonism between the British and Americans as the latter accused the host judges of discrimination against the professionalism of their approach. The result was that the British – for the first and only time – managed to win more medals than the Americans. Despite this it was felt that the home teams had underperformed, some attributing this to the strictly amateur approach whilst others denigrated 'those who make a business of sport'.

The English sporting establishment was slowly but surely forced to make a choice between the amateur (recreational) approach, in which winning was not that important, and a more professional approach, in which winning was of prime importance.

Governing bodies continued to follow the amateur way even though the international trend was in the opposite direction. Further failure at the Stockholm Olympics in 1912 caused widespread anxiety, with some British team members not happy with 'the way in which affairs have been managed … and appear ridiculous by contrast to the perfect organisation of the Americans'.

There were immediate calls for the professionalisation of training, organisation and funding of British teams but by 1920 and the Antwerp Olympics a leading sports administrator was seriously advising withdrawal from the Olympic movement.

Theodore Cook, the most influential sports administrator in England at the time, wrote the letter below:

> **This country has made it perfectly clear that the whole Olympic movement has become entirely alien to English thought and character. England has utterly refused to give our representatives sufficient money to give them any chance of showing their best form. The Secretary of the British Olympic Committee should inform the International Olympic Committee that this country will not be represented at any future games and so say farewell to the Olympic movement as it is presently conducted.**

Whilst the tone of Cook's letter might give the impression that he was trying to blackmail the government into giving more money to the cause of winning at international sport, it was generally taken as a plea against creeping professionalism in the Games.

Given Cook's social, cultural and sporting background this would be the obvious conclusion to draw but the letter was vigorously repudiated by others that followed and which made the point that English sport had to change or die.

The Secretary of the British Olympic Committee and forty-five members of the British team considered the professional approach as the only way to competitive success.

This approach reached its climax at the Berlin Olympics in 1936 where the Third Reich registered its sporting domination using techniques of trialling and selection that were later adopted and improved upon by communist countries of the eastern bloc. Some of these methods were ethically and morally highly questionable.

The inflexibility of governing bodies over the definition of amateurism allied to the xenophobia of the English gentleman produced a tension in international sporting relations that still has repercussions today and to which we shall return in Chapter Eight.

Domestically, the continued application of the amateur ethic, particularly during the nineteenth century, was directly responsible for the formation of hundreds of clubs throughout the country which were established either to maintain social exclusivity or provide a means by which those excluded could carry on with their own independently organised activities. It is to the fortunes of these clubs that we shall turn in the next chapter.

TABLE 6.1   Sports development by social status

Era	High social status	Social division maintained by	Low social status
13th century to 18th century	Master, lord, landowner, aristocrat, gentry	Royal proclamation, civil law, bye-laws, game laws, commercial pressure	Man, peasant, tenant, servant, employee
Early 19th century.	Gentleman Leisure used as badge of social superiority Pure amateur (no money)	Taking over and gentrifying sport, including working men in subservient positions	Working man Leisure used as a rest from work Quasi-amateur (money in prizes and expenses)
Mid-19th century	New gentlemen in public schools and suburban recreation	Withdrawal into recreation and away from 'open' competition	Pseudo professional (broken-time payments)
Late 19th century	Establishment of gentlemanly amateur governing bodies Clubs for gentlemen amateurs only	Redefining 'amateur' and enforcing exclusion through 'blackballing' and high cost	Establishment of alternative governing bodies and clubs for tradesmen amateurs (prizes only) and professionals (wages)
20th century (up to World War II)	Upper/middle class	Social divisions remain but governing bodies encouraged co-operation due to international competition	Working class
20th century (post-World War II)	Socio-economic groups A, B and C	The Sports Council (1965) imposes a 'sport for all' policy	Socio-economic groups D and E

AMATEURISM

1   What is the difference between 'gentlemanly pursuits' and 'peasant recreations'?

2   Using cricket as an example, explain what is meant by the terms 'appropriation' and 'gentrification'.

3   What was 'broken time' and why was it that association football was not torn apart by this issue as was the case in rugby?

4   What was the 'mechanics' clause' and what were its consequences?

5   It has been suggested that the definition of 'amateur sport' was in fact based on social acceptability and that the issue of money was simply a smokescreen – discuss.

6   How did the growth of Olympism and international sport influence 'amateur views' on sport in England?

Suggested further reading

Lowerson, J., *Sport and the English Middle Classes* (Manchester University Press, 1993)

Mason, A., *Association Football and English Society, 1863–1915* (Harvester Press, 1980)

Perkin, H., *The Origins of Modern English Society, 1780–1880* (Routledge, 1969)

chapter seven

CLUB FORTUNES

John O'Gaunt Bowmen, established 1604, revived 1788, 1869 and 1977.

(From page 1 of the current minute book)

All sport brought to a halt.

(Headline in **The Daily Mail,** *Sepember 4th, 1939)*

It is apparent over a period of centuries that club fortunes have been affected by an enormous variety of factors. These include the obvious considerations of geography and environment, social cultures, politics and economics to club constitution and administration, each of which may have helped or hindered club progress.

During the eighteenth century, for example, Manchester and Liverpool 'sucked in such a mass of population from other regions that the whole demographic balance of the country was upset'. A result of this was that many rural sports were introduced to an urban location for the first time outside London.

Increasingly convenient travel stimulated growth outside London and significantly the word 'provinces' only came into the language in the 1780s to identify the divide between the country and the capital city. London had long been criticised for monopolising commercial activity to the disadvantage of the rest of the country.

During the 1870s it became obvious that the provinces were asserting their claim to a more important place in national development and that much of this assertiveness came from working people. The Factory Act of 1878 had awarded ordinary folk a free Saturday afternoon which was being filled with recreational activity of all types including sporting participation and spectatorship.

Some employers, like Beyer Peacock of Gorton in Manchester, encouraged the formation of recreational clubs at work and joint championships were organised between factories, mills and commercial businesses. Many became annual events such as the Manchester Business Houses Cross-Country Championships held in Heaton Park every year until the 1930s.

It was the development of such grass-roots organisations that led to the regional associations and leagues that gradually replaced the London governing bodies as the focus of sporting activity.

It was during the 1870s that a stricter definition of social class came into being and the easier identification of 'working class' simply served to isolate the growing middle classes who chose to live out of town in the new 'suburbia'.

Sport, class and money

The new middle-class money encouraged the spread of recreation as demonstrated by the huge increase in the number of sports clubs in suburban areas for those who had the time and money to utilise them fully.

In Birmingham, for example, the suburb of Edgbaston was established as a result of the middle class moving there to avoid 'the artisan belt encircling the city'. Several cricket and tennis clubs were formed and became well supported and prosperous in no time at all.

There was some debate in the national press, particularly *The Daily Telegraph*, about the benefits of such recreational indulgence since critics suggested that such 'idleness' was socially damaging. Others thought that sport was character building.

Whilst the growth of middle-class sport was evidenced by the growth of club memberships, in working-class culture it was much more evident in increasing levels of spectatorship. This may have been due to the reluctance of working people to tire themselves further after working hard throughout the week, or because, until 1902, they (at least officially) had no physical education at school, which might have encouraged them to take part.

Just as economic prosperity bolstered interest in recreational activity, economic depression produced a proportionate decline. Many early sporting clubs, having been formed by friends who purchased shares and promised to pay debts, were often badly affected by economic downturn.

Each of the twenty original subscribers to the Fulwood Race Course near Preston were asked to give £15 in 1786 but were very soon encouraged to add a further

£10 to cover substantial losses of over £300 in 1790. By 1794 the races had been cancelled but by 1803 when the economic problems caused by the Napoleonic Wars had been largely solved, a dividend of 30 per cent was paid out to the remaining shareholders.

During the same period, a similar fluctuation could be seen in Darlington where the local archery society was compelled to levy a surcharge of five shillings per member to ensure the continuation of the association.

Decline and depression

A further decline set in during the 1870s with a great industrial depression that lasted – with minor upturns – until 1896. The Staffordshire Bowmen were forced to reduce their activities from three meetings a season to two since otherwise 'expenses would be rather heavy' and the Headingley Bowling Club's membership figures reflect the economic depression, falling from 112 to 54.

The Astley Bowling Club was unable to pay the rent on its ground for several years in the 1880s due to arrears in subscriptions caused by unemployment. The Tyldesley Swimming Club was forced to abandon its annual festivals 'due to the disastrous state of trade'. Many clubs, like the Tyldesley Cricket Club in 1889, appointed a collector of subscriptions on 10 per cent commission, but even this drastic type of action often failed to save clubs from extinction. Many, like the Irthing Vale Cricket Club in 1874, decided to cease activities and re-establish at a later date when economic conditions improved.

Some clubs struggled through bad times with a much reduced membership and competitive activity. One was the Appleby Golf Club in Westmorland, which suffered a serious decline in membership during the 1890s, so that by 1899 it could boast only fifteen women and twenty men subscribers. Like many other clubs it managed to continue by amalgamating with a neighbouring club and securing vital cost and efficiency gains.

The new century failed to produce greater prosperity with a brief upturn immediately followed by thirty years of economic depression and stagnation. All of this was reflected in club development:

- Lancaster Golf Club had '500 fewer visitors'
- Bolton Rugby Union Club disbanded, owing to the extreme difficulty of raising a team

- Kendal Ladies Hockey Club could not afford to rent a field and folded in 1911

- South Saxon Archers were disbanded in 1932 due to 'altered economic circumstances'

- Warrington Anglers Association suffered its worst ever season 'because of unemployment"

… and so on across the country and with every sport being affected.

Such hard times did, however, have some benefits for boxing since the 1930s was a golden age at professional level as new talent flowed from the dole queues into the sport. Desperate to make a living, many men became involved in (often) dubiously managed commercial bouts in the larger industrial cities, particularly Manchester, that excited great interest from increasingly sophisticated audiences.

Sport broadens its horizons

The growth of industrialisation and of large urban populations was facilitated by the continued extension of the railway system. This encouraged the development of towns and cities and allowed those who lived in them to escape easily to other areas for a whole range of recreational purposes.

The effect that such ease of movement had on the growth of sporting events can be seen relatively early in the history of the railways as people moved out of town to row, play cricket, hunt and race horses. In hunting particularly it became possible in the 1840s to spend easy weekends in Oxfordshire when the railways first opened up the Thames Valley and Birmingham routes. Rail travel reached Leicester in the 1850s and was much used by Anthony Trollope, who began to hunt there in 1851.

We have seen that the new rail service to Liverpool in 1837 was commended by Lord Greville for the convenience with which it transported him to the races and reference to the *Racing Calendar* for any date in 1840 shows an enormous range of meetings, most of which had become accessible by rail from London. On April 28th of that year, for example, there were thirty-six race meetings around the country, of which thirty-three were newly accessible by railway.

At a local level 'derby' games between close neighbours were made much easier by the new rail networks. The Whitfield Cricket Club in Northumberland, for instance, could catch any train on the Tyne Valley line to travel to all its fifteen away fixtures, with the return matches reached just as easily by their opponents.

Elsewhere other forms of transport made life considerably easier for local sport. The new Bolton Union Football Club, established in 1904, chose its playing field because it was conveniently situated for the local tramway terminus and its accessibility for all the members.

Enter the car ...

Later in the century, cars became commonplace; at least for the better off. The effect on the sport of golf was fairly evident since many of the new courses were sited beyond the range of public transport (and of course, any 'undesirable elements').

Hunting, according to Lady Augusta Fane in her book, *Chit Chat* (1926), was spoiled by motorcars, since they allowed 'a crowd of strangers to hunt where they do not live and where they consequently spend no money'. Nevertheless, cars did have their uses in transporting hunt members to remote meets and in providing followers with a means of keeping up with the chase. This could often be useful as it was for the North Staffordshire Hounds in January 1927 when a rider fell heavily from his horse 'and was taken to hospital by car'.

Until cars were more widely available after World War II most sports club outings were by charabanc (motor coach) and the Netherfield Swimming Club of Kendal exemplified this in its regular Monday trips to Lancaster baths for training: 'leaving at 6.30 p.m. and returning at 9.00 p.m. sharp; one shilling for seniors and nothing for juniors'.

Everything in its rightful place

Many factors determining fluctuations in club fortunes were peculiar to the sport involved. For example, a public handbill published in the *Birmingham Gazette* of April 1790 illustrated how the local Wolverhampton Hunt suffered in a way that has become peculiar to hunting. Mr Gough, a landowner, upset that the hunt had ridden over his property, 'laid a foil and drew a drag over his grounds' to attract the hunt into a compound where he tried 'to destroy the hounds with a large stick'. Naturally he failed and the huntsmen published the handbill to publicise their judgement on him as 'contemptible in the Field as he is in every other part of his character'; which was the type that disliked the establishment and all authority.

Although the role of hunt saboteur did not develop until 1945, the hunting fraternity had plenty of other problems to confront, not least of which was the destruction of habitat and over-killing, which meant fewer foxes being caught and killed.

The Stayley Hunt decided, at a General Meeting in September 1904, that it should disband 'due to the over-killing of foxes by non-members of the hunt who use lurcher dogs to do so'. Elsewhere, the spread of towns drastically reduced the opportunities for hunting. Cosmo Gordon Lang's *Sermons* (1913) recall Lord Berkeley's huntsman, as early as the end of the eighteenth century, following a fox at Wormwood Scrubs only to lose him in the newly built Kensington Gardens development.

The general availability of foxes was maintained by assiduous planting of shrubs and bushes for their protection. This was done by the Marquis Cholmondeley in Norfolk during the 1830s and seemed to have worked since the number of foxes killed remained fairly constant over the years. The North Staffordshire Hounds killed sixty-seven foxes in 1877 and eighty-six in 1927 but each year had many days when there was 'no scent and no foxes'.

Local economic depression effectively killed off horse racing in places like Lancaster, where in the 1850s subscriptions dried up completely. Like hunting, horse racing was affected by the availability of suitable venues. Whilst much early racing was restricted or terminated by the enclosure of land during the eighteenth and nineteenth centuries, urban development later played its part in reducing the number of available venues.

In Lancaster, the old racecourse on Quay Meadow became warehousing in the eighteenth century and the new course on Lancaster Moor was too remote for popular use. This, together with the decline in trade and prosperity brought about the death of racing there in 1858.

At Fulwood in Preston the original course (1786) was substantially improved initially only to be bought by speculators during the mid-nineteenth century and covered with suburban Victorian villas. Similarly a descendant of the original owner moved the course at Newton-le-Willows (1678) from Newton Common to Haydock Park (1897) when the Common became ripe for commercial development.

The costs of developing sporting facilities often brought clubs close to bankruptcy and bore particularly heavily on those sports which were dependent upon ground maintenance for their existence.

Bowling, with its reliance on well-tended greens, suffered periodically when the bowling surface needed replacing, renovating or extending. In 1793 the Didsbury Bowling Green committee employed Joseph Kelsall for forty-eight days to enlarge their green and paid out £36 12s 9d in order to maintain it for that one season. Whilst this was an enormous expense, it was proportionally no greater than the

£220 paid by the Trowbridge and Westbourne Recreation Club for the same task in 1921. This resulted in a similar increase in membership and subscription income to that experienced in Didsbury.

In the early days of cricket it was common for urban grounds to be enclosed at considerable cost in order to produce a secure arena. Even rural clubs would try to enclose their grounds with canvas sheeting, partly to limit the playing area and partly to control spectators and charge entry fees.

Such control continued to be necessary throughout the nineteenth century and even small clubs like Tyldesley Cricket Club in Lancashire required 255 yards of wooden boarding eight feet high to surround its ground in 1884. This was the club's first year of competition in the local league and this brought with it a responsibility for large crowds of spectators. The Lancashire League demanded a better playing surface and so some 4,000 square yards of turf was re-laid at a cost that could only be redeemed by the (anticipated) income from greater numbers of spectators.

Golf and tennis were also faced with the difficulties of maintaining expensive facilities, the cost of which were often beyond the financial scope of smaller clubs. The Appleby Golf Club (minutes of November 8th, 1903), which eventually amalgamated with a neighbouring club, was helped in its decline by 'the farmer turning out his cattle, which did great damage to the putting surfaces, making them unplayable all summer'.

In tennis, uneven grass surfaces as well as the earliest artificial surfaces of rolled earth and crushed stone, were liable to produce ankle-turning lumps and bumps. Bad weather often caused great expense to smaller clubs, so that following incessant rain and frost the Dunmow Park Tennis Club was forced to have its playing surfaces re-laid. This, together with a reduced membership forced the club to organise proper matches against the clubs at Saffron Walden, Ongar, Felstead and Chelmsford for the first time in order to raise money in match-fees.

Such problems did not affect the Wimbledon club. Its profits soared from £0 1s 10d in 1879 to £760 in 1881 as the lawn tennis championships became established there. Despite economic depressions, the Wimbledon club was able to afford a new pavilion costing £1,200 in 1899 when it was re-titled the All England Lawn Tennis and Croquet Club. It went from strength to strength and became an increasingly fashionable sporting venue.

Whilst facilities could be major liabilities, the fact that they *were* provided was a major cause of the growth of sport and in some cases its very inception. Advances in cycle production followed by the construction of artificial tracks took cycling from being a pure recreation into the realm of organised competitive activity. Similarly, the provision of baths for washing and plunge pools for swimming by local councils, following the Baths and Wash-houses Act of 1846, created a huge upsurge in the popularity of both recreational and competitive swimming.

In Manchester, the Mayfield pool, opened in 1856, created a demand for recreational swimming with the Mayfield Swimming Club very soon established. The Osborne SC was formed when the Osborne pool was opened in 1883, and a public meeting following the opening of the new baths in Warrington in 1893 called for the formation of a swimming club with forty members paying 2/6d (12½ p) each.

During the same year Stockport Council stated their intention to provide 'a first-class swimming bath eighty feet by thirty feet, a small swimming bath for ladies and some private baths for the labouring classes', which soon resulted in the establishment of swimming clubs for men and women.

Playing for money

Internal tensions produced varying fortunes in the major winter games of association football and rugby union football in the north as the principles of amateurism were gradually eroded in both codes. Rugby Union had arrived in Lancashire in 1857 when a Mr Mather organised a match in Liverpool and Richard Sykes, a former captain of Rugby School, established the first Manchester Club in 1860.

In Yorkshire, the Headingley and Wakefield clubs set the 'amateur' tone with ex-public schoolboys being joined by others from old established schools such as Leeds Grammar and Queen Elizabeth's Grammar in Wakefield. Smaller amateur clubs such as Bolton were less fortunate with their recruitment and attracted enthusiastic novices rather than trained traditionalists. Consequently the club suffered socially, competitively and financially.

As a different social element began to play rugby it was necessary to modify some of the amateur principles in order to cater for working-class needs. The split with the Rugby Union came as a result of the formation of the Lancashire and Yorkshire Leagues in 1892 and led inevitably to the formation of the Northern Union in 1895.

This had a devastating effect, especially in the more industrialised Lancashire, where most of the strongest clubs left the Lancashire Rugby Union to join the Northern Union, which was prepared to condone broken-time payments. The split served to polarise the amateur and quasi-amateur elements in the sport and clubs identified themselves with one or the other. Particular areas became known as 'league' or 'union' country.

As broken-time payments evolved into wages for part-time professionals, the temptation 'to go north' for poorly paid or unemployed union players was overwhelming. Particularly during times of depression there was a mass exodus of players to the northern league clubs. Between 1919 and 1926 forty rugby union internationals, mostly from Wales, 'went north'.

Although the progress of professionalism in association football had been similar to that in rugby, the dominance of the professional code was established far more quickly than had been the case in the oval ball game. The Football Association was established in 1863 as an amateur body with amateur aspirations and yet the growth of the sport in the northern industrial areas soon brought about a rift with the governing body, which refused to accept any payment being made to players.

County Football Associations were formed in 1878, some of which allowed quasi-amateurs to play and regional competitions led to regular payments as the gate money increased.

Full professionalisation came with the formation of the Football League in 1888. This was established by William McGregor of the Aston Villa Football Club who saw the commercial potential of a competition restricted to several major teams – in this case twelve of the largest clubs. The original clubs all represented towns with a population of 80,000 or more – enough spectators and gate money to make it financially viable. The 'magnificent 12' were:

- Accrington Stanley
- Aston Villa
- Blackburn Rovers
- Bolton Wanderers
- Burnley
- Derby County
- Everton
- Nottingham County
- Preston North End
- Stoke City
- West Bromwich Albion
- Wolverhampton Wanderers.

All of these clubs, 119 years later, with the exception of Accrington Stanley, remain in the Football League and almost half of them are still in the top division – a remarkable achievement in the fast-changing world of football.

A second division was soon added to the original and other regional leagues sprang up so that many clubs became substantial businesses. In 1899, Tottenham Hotspur FC – not even in the first division of the Southern League – gambled on a twenty-one year lease on a ground behind the White Hart Inn. According to the shareholders' prospectus, the enclosure 'will be a very fine one capable of accommodating 25,000 spectators with 2,000 seated under cover'. Eight thousand shares were offered at a pound each, of which 1,626 were sold in the first year. This was enough for work to start and that same year over £7,000 was taken in gate money, set against nearly £4,000 paid out in players' wages.

Tottenham were certainly not the only club to invest heavily. The league system of competition encouraged spectator support to such an extent (because of the excitement of promotion and relegation) that between 1889 and 1910 fifty-eight clubs moved into new larger grounds. By 1910, 1 million people a year paid to watch First Division football alone.

The Tottenham club's enterprise paid off. They won the FA Cup in 1901 and despite the financial hardships of World War I the club's seventeenth Annual Report in 1915 said that 'there is no reason why the company should not make substantial profits as in the past'.

The Professional Footballers' Association was established as a Players' Union in 1898 and complained that such profits should result in higher wages for the players. However, the club chairmen collectively found a way of keeping wages down by establishing the principle of a maximum wage. This was not finally abolished until 1961!

Meanwhile, the huge gap between the professional and amateur sides of the sport can best be appreciated by looking at a typical village club. The Kinson FC in Dorset was forced to reduce its subscriptions from 1/6d to 1/– in order to boost membership in the same year that Tottenham was spending thousands of pounds to build its grandstand.

The club had joined the Dorset FA for further competition and support in 1898 and debated the possibility of joining the Hampshire FA, only to conclude that 'the club was hardly in a sufficiently forward position to embark on such a large venture'. This gap between the 'haves' and the 'have nots' in football continues to the present day and will be looked at in Chapter Nine.

Making profits and covering losses

Irrespective of size or persuasion, many sports clubs had viability problems which were often solved by joining or associating with others. We have already seen that the original Lancaster Rowing Club (1842) was initially a cricket club and the process in reverse was accomplished at Warwick when its boat club evolved into a tennis and bowling club in 1927.

The Appleby Golf Club was only one of many that joined with a neighbouring club (1903) in order to remain financially viable and this happened across the sporting spectrum. Some of many examples follow:

- 1865 – Wood Green Cricket Club (Essex) joined with Crouch End CC
- 1877 – Netherfield Swimming Club diversified into gymnastics (Kendal)
- 1884 – Tyldesley Cricket Club (Lancs.) joined with the local tennis club
- 1884 – Huyton Cricket Club (Liverpool) associated with Huyton Hockey Club
- 1886 – Lewisham Hare and Hounds Club formed a cycling section
- 1900 – Kendal Ladies Hockey Club associated with Kendal Girls High School
- 1905 – Eight rugby clubs in Kendal form the Kendal Rugby Union Football Club
- 1907 – Derwent Rowing Club (Derby) started a football section
- 1908 – Blackheath Cricket Club started a hockey section
- 1913 – Herne Hill Harriers established a cycling section.

We can see from the variety of sports in the above list that clubs around the country were vulnerable to fluctuations of fortune. This required them to be adaptable and often an attachment to some more prosperous body was the way in which a struggling club managed to continue.

Sunningdale Ladies Golf Club, which enjoyed a close relationship with the men's club, and the Dunmow Tennis Club, which actually moved its premises to a more prosperous area in order to improve its membership and subscription income, are examples of such adaptability.

The Headingley Bowling Club arranged to continue its activities at the Original Oak public house, whilst the Warrington Anglers Association joined the National Federation of Anglers, claiming that the Federation 'would give protection against any further attempts at interference from rival bodies'.

Fashionable sports

To the fluctuations of fortune and their causes must be added the element of fashion and changing custom, which greatly affected participation in sport.

In 1773 William Hickey justified his declining interest in rowing by explaining that 'rowing ceased to be the fashion and was supplanted by sailing'. In 1801 Strutt, in his *Sports and Pastimes of the People of England*, mentioned that football, 'although formerly in vogue has now fallen into disrepute and is but little practised'.

Certainly, during the nineteenth century there was a disproportionate decrease in participation as spectatorship increased and as we have seen, 1 million people a year paid to watch First Division football by 1910 whilst local amateur clubs struggled to field a team at weekends.

This relative change from participation to spectating was particularly noticeable amongst the working class as sport became less of a recreation and more of an entertainment. At the same time the middle-class participation levels actually increased, evidence of which is clear in the phenomenal growth of membership in sports most associated with that class.

In 1850 England had one golf club but by 1914 there were 200 catering for a social élite amongst which, it has to be said, snobbery, sexism and anti-Semitism were common.

In tennis there were 300 clubs affiliated to the Lawn Tennis Association in 1900 but by 1937 this had grown to 3,000; an explosion explained by the construction of 3 million private houses in suburbia since 1920.

In Leeds a policy of Jewish exclusion resulted in the large Jewish community establishing its own club (Moor Allerton) in 1932 – which nevertheless welcomed gentile members.

In an era when football and rugby were beginning to attract large crowds, horse racing was also coming back into fashion, especially in the south of England. New rules of racing were introduced in 1858 and revised in 1868 and 1871 to ensure fair contests. In 1883 the sport had become so popular that the increase in the number of race meetings was checked due to lack of space in the racing calendar.

By 1880 cricket had also become a mass entertainment with crowds in excess of 15,000 attending county matches and many more going to the 'Test' matches, the first of which was played between England and Australia in 1877 in Melbourne. *The Times* of May 20th, 1882, in a leading article, contended that the Tests were a 'wholesome innovation' but criticised the tendency of spectators to regard them as 'simply opportunities to observe displays of individual skill by cricketing stars'.

From the 1880s to the 1950s cricket was generally regarded as the English national game and attracted mass attendances into the late 1940s. However, the advent of other attractions (sporting and otherwise) saw crowds at county games dwindle – often to minute proportions – by the mid-1950s.

The popularity of one activity sometimes directly influenced others as we saw with William Hickey's rowing and sailing. For example:

- 1820s – a decline in race meetings led to a revival of Cumberland wrestling
- 1880s – a decline in archery was balanced by growth in golf and tennis
- 1890s – cycling was overtaken by boating, tennis and rambling as 'fashionable' activities
- 1930s – dog racing supplanted horse racing for many working people
- 1940s – quoits and pitch and toss played on streets gave way to bowling on public house greens
- 1950s – many working-class recreations in towns were supplanted by fishing in the countryside.

Sport and World War I

There remains one last important determinant of club fortunes which influences all the others – and that is war. War affects society in many different ways. It:

- alters the cultural and commercial climate
- causes huge economic and demographic upheavals
- curtails civilian movements
- modifies social and sexual stereotyping
- speeds up the rate of technological progress.

All of the above have an effect on sport at club level. Eighteenth-century sport was often described as 'manly, noble and patriotic' as it was thought that it prepared participants for military service. Pugilism was cited as evidence that the true born Englishman had the determination and pugnacity to defend the realm against any foreign threat and even the popularity of cock-fighting and bull-baiting was held to illustrate the combative nature of the ordinary man in the street. Some activities were praised as particularly useful 'schools' for future conscripts to the armed forces, including:

- archery: which trained people for work as infantrymen until the seventeenth century

- rowing: which helped to prepare people for service in the navy throughout the seventeenth and eighteenth centuries

- riding and hunting: which in the nineteenth century was considered to be excellent training for the cavalry.

Thames watermen were frequently 'pressed' or forced into military service simply by being kidnapped and taken on board ship against their will. A famous example was John Taylor who lived from 1580 to 1654 and who was 'pressed' into the navy on no fewer than seven occasions but being more fortunate than most ended his life as a prosperous publican in Oxford.

The first war to have a noticeable effect on club culture was the Boer War, which went on intermittently around the end of the nineteenth century and the beginning of the twentieth. When men offered themselves for service and were given the routine physical checks it was found that so few were actually fit for military service that there was a scandal concerning 'the deterioration of the national physique'.

The physical tests on Manchester volunteers during October 1899 found that of 10,000 men only 2,000 were remotely fit and even they were not fit enough for combat duties.

It is worth pointing out that the healthy volunteers were those who regularly took part in sport and so a disproportionately high percentage of successful recruits were members of sports clubs. Confirmation of this can be found in members' lists and casualty figures not only for the Boer War period but also for subsequent hostilities. It has been said, and was demonstrably true, that sports clubs were 'breeders of patriotism'.

Whilst educational reform sought to remedy these defects by introducing physical education into state schools for the first time, the National Rifle Association, established in 1860 for the 'encouragement of the Volunteer Rifle Corps', issued a memorandum on January 16th, 1900 designed to promote the training of more riflemen. This resulted in large numbers of applications to form local rifle clubs, a condition often being that each club must have at least twenty members and that rifles were to be issued on a ratio of one for every ten members. The civil authorities exempted members from payment of firearms licences and the council of the National Rifle Association believed that the scheme would be 'a fruitful source of valuable recruits to Her Majesty's forces'.

Many of the clubs passed on members to local rifle corps, and these in turn supplied the army units that had been re-organised in 1881 on a territorial basis. Most of these clubs were typical of Casterton Rifle Club of Westmorland, which was established 'to promote instruction and practice in the use of the rifle' and attracted twenty members at 1/– entrance fee and 1/– annual subscription. Membership numbers increased immediately before both world wars but by the end of the 1950s support collapsed. On June 10th, 1965 the club was wound up and members were advised to 'join the Sedbergh Rifle Club'.

World War I had, as might be imagined, an enormous effect upon English sport at every level. Just before its outbreak county cricket clubs began their games on Wednesdays and Saturdays instead of Mondays and Thursday in order to attract bigger crowds; for as *The Times* of May 4th, 1914 put it, 'people in these mercantile days want a big return for their money and a quick decision of the game draws the money'.

A few months later Dr Grace wrote in *The Sportsman* of August 27th, 1914 that:

> **The fighting on the continent is very severe and I think the time has come when the cricket season should be brought to a close for it is not fitting at a time like this that able bodied men should be playing day after day and pleasure seekers looking on.**

This abrupt end to professional cricket was repeated in the amateur game as members joined up in their thousands leaving juniors and veterans to look after the interests of clubs in their absence. At Irthing Vale Cricket Club a groundsman was employed to keep the square in good condition although no play took place at all during 1916, 1917 or 1918. Similar situations prevailed at Huyton CC in Liverpool, at Durham CC and at Kempsford CC in Gloucestershire.

Several years of sporting inactivity coupled with a continuation of social activities (albeit at a lower level than usual) often resulted in a healthy financial situation when the clubs returned to normality in 1919 or 1920. At Huyton the fixture list was arranged as far as possible using the same clubs and dates as in 1914 and 'everything was to be put in first class order as there were many new members likely to join'. This was said in the knowledge that the funds to do so were available.

At Durham thirty new members joined in 1919 and the annual report records a substantial balance of funds, which was vitally necessary since 'the ground needed to be brought up to its pre-war condition'. At Kempsford there were thirty-four new members in 1919, deriving income of £11 14s 0d, a considerable improvement on pre-war levels.

Missing in action

In the early months of the war, prior to conscription, when the British forces consisted largely of volunteers, sports clubs tended to supply a disproportionate number of men for front-line action. This can be seen in the mortality rates commemorated in Rolls of Honour in every single club. At Huyton CC fifty-six members joined up and ten died; at Durham CC forty-five joined up and six died; at Kempsford the numbers were twenty and four, respectively and at Irthing Vale ten joined up with two subsequent fatalities.

These figures represented a mortality rate of 17 per cent (approximately one death per six men who joined up) and were sustained between 1914 and 1916. In 1917 *Wisden* published no less than sixty pages of obituaries, finally recording the deaths in 1919 of sixty leading exponents of the first-class game. In the clubs mentioned in this book the mortality rate during World War I approaches one in five.

This really only tells half the story, since hundreds of thousands of men returned from the conflict who were incapable of taking part in sport: mainly due to gas poisoning. The majority of sports clubs of necessity became youth orientated and women began to join clubs in ever-increasing numbers. There were often more women members than men in cycling, swimming, tennis and golf clubs in the 1920s.

The association football season had just started when the war broke out but instead of abandoning play, as happened in other sports, the football authorities let it continue. This caused extremely unfavourable press comments and a loss of reputation for the game that lasted for a full twenty years. This was based on the perception that those involved in the game were only interested in making money and lacked patriotism.

Many public schools (the last bastions of patriotism) dropped football as a result of this perception and took up rugby instead: it being more widely seen as the game for patriotic gentlemen. The Northern Rugby League Football Union took notice of the adverse press comments and pronounced that 'excepting for schoolboys and juniors under eighteen, all competitive football under Northern Union rules be suspended for the duration of the war'.

By the end of the war *The Times*, September 25th, 1919, at least had come to realise that 'the round ball did more than anything else to revive tired limbs and weary minds. Everyone knows that association football is the game that soldiers and sailors love best'. This particular quotation goes on to make the point that 'the authorities should devote particular attention to the training of officers of the future in the game that their men will play' and it was true that there was a growth of interest in sport across the social divide during World War II.

The authorities were far more disposed to encourage sporting activities during World War II as a means of boosting morale; and this was one of the determinants of a much greater democratisation in sport and wider society which can be seen after 1945.

The football business obviously suffered through declining gates and there was a proposal for a reduction in players' wages in order 'to assist the financially weaker clubs, since all workers were having to sacrifice in a similar manner'.

An indication of the loss of business can be found in the annual report of the Tottenham Hotspur Football and Athletic Company for 1915, which states that 'since the war receipts are 65% lower than normal and the loss has been £3,968'. Play continued in a restricted form with 'friendlies' and charity matches and the club played its part by raising £1,000 towards various war charities. The temptation to carry on paying players at the full rate with bonuses in order to keep a winning team was considerable and at least one First Division club, Leeds City FC, was banned from all competition in 1919 and re-surfaced as Leeds United in 1920.

At amateur level play continued in a fairly chaotic way with teams of juniors and veterans fulfilling local fixtures. The Kinson FC in Dorset, like many others, established a junior club to see it through the hostilities and planned practice nights, as much to maintain morale as to improve technique.

The Professional Footballers' Union became defunct during the war due to lack of subscription income leaving liabilities of over £700. However, when it revived in 1919 it had a much higher level of subscriptions and this allowed it to represent its members from a position of greater strength. Negotiations with club chairmen resulted in a small rise in wages, a share in transfer fees and a winning bonus scheme, whilst the union officers managed to organise financial aid for relatives of members killed or injured.

The union also provided comprehensive legal advice for its members and its 1919 annual report concluded that 'there was no reason why the Union should not be ten times as strong and the officers mean to have it so'. Unfortunately there was no insurance possible for those who lost their lives in the war or who were injured since no insurer could have afforded to pay the sums involved. Eighty of the game's leading players were killed in the conflict.

In the years immediately prior to the war, bowling clubs had been worried about the succession of wet winters followed by very dry springs which played havoc with playing surfaces. Nevertheless, the lovely summers helped to boost memberships and the Moseley Bowling Club's annual report for 1913 concluded that 'the very first concern of a bowling club is the weather, which has been exceedingly good, resulting in a large increase in membership and a record income from championships'.

Whilst the onset of war caused cancellations of inter-club matches, most clubs continued to function at a basic level since their largely middle-aged membership remained untouched by conscription until 1917 when even they were called up to help in the 'final push' for victory.

Little mention of the war is found in club minutes except for the odd allusion to 'the circumstances of the times', usually cited to justify some relaxation of usual procedures. This was the case at the Headingley club where 'subscriptions be allowed to lapse'.

In March 1917, the Westbourne Recreation Club committee felt 'that the nation had a greater claim on the groundsman's services than the club', whilst in August of the same year the Headingley club was mourning the loss of its groundsman who died from gas poisoning and was 'our first loss in this great war'.

The records of clubs show no large fluctuations of fortune during the war years although some simply left a gap from 1915 to 1920.

After the war, most clubs record a Peace Day Championship, held in the summer of 1919, to which there was always 'a splendid muster which turned up to compete'.

Immediately after the war everything was done to return to normality as quickly as possible. Fixture lists were re-established, subscriptions set at pre-war levels and membership numbers soon returned to – even exceeded – those of 1914. This was largely due to the retention of middle-aged and elderly members liberally supplemented by juniors. The sport of bowling, unlike some others, remained a female-free zone.

The war encouraged women's participation in swimming. In 1916 Bolton Swimming Club had 87 men, 116 boys, 89 women and 50 girls enrolled as members. The large male membership was due to the fact that the club had allowed all soldiers and sailors free membership so that they could enjoy the baths when on leave. Nevertheless, by 1918 40 per cent of the club's membership still consisted of women – uncommon for most swimming clubs.

The Warrington club was unusual in that it almost folded during the war apart from issuing a few reduced price season tickets for schoolboys. Much other sporting activity in the town also came to a halt due, as the minutes of the Anglers' Association record, to 'the large number of members who responded to the call to arms and the suffering of those in want of employment consequent to the war'.

Around the country other sports also curtailed their activities; either of necessity or a desire to show solidarity with the armed forces overseas. For example:

- October 1914 – Darlington Cycling Club decided 'in the present state of affairs it would not be advisable to do anything'
- March 1915 – Hammersmith Sailing Club closed 'until further notice'
- Dunmow Park Tennis Club closed for the duration of the hostilities
- Sunningdale Ladies' Golf Club ceased playing but worked for the Queen's 'Work for Women Fund.'

World War II

If discontinuation of sporting activity typified the reaction to World War I, then a dogged determination to 'carry on regardless' was the general response to World War II.

Despite initial panic, during which the FA cancelled players' contracts, cut wages to 30/– a week and limited crowds to 8,000, the game was soon reorganised into a system of district competitions. Unlike the activities during the first war, these district competitions were given both popular and official approval since it was felt that they helped to keep the communal spirits up. The suspension of bonus money for winning and league championship points actually resulted in high scoring matches and excellent football; a lesson that was learned during the war only to be abandoned afterwards in the name of commercialisation and professionalisation.

An FA circular of April 1939 expressed the hope that the game would provide a patriotic example to the youth of the country and, indeed, clubs like West Ham United and Bolton Wanderers encouraged their whole playing staffs to enlist.

This attitude was undoubtedly informed by the bitter memories of the Great War when football had been accused of being unpatriotic. The FA and the Players' Union agreed that 'the professional footballer is determined to carry on this great game for the benefit of the community in spite of the threats made by evil minded dictators to weaken the morale of the people'.

Early reports during the first months of the war declared that the outbreak of hostilities had shattered many sports organisations due to an absence of a policy of transformation to a wartime situation. A contemporary survey showed that 70 per cent of the people no longer took part in sport due to lack of time and money as well as the difficulties of travel.

During the 'phoney war' (the early days of World War II) restrictions were placed on crowd sizes at sporting venues but by the middle of 1940 football clubs were allowed to fill their grounds to half capacity. Birmingham City FC was allowed to open its ground following a *Birmingham Post* (March 26th, 1940) campaign which declared that 'the Germans are foul and dirty fighters but even they could hardly be expected to choose Saturday afternoon as the time and City's football ground as the locale for their first manifestation of frightfulness'.

As hostilities wore on, public support for the continuation of football held firm, although there was strong feeling that horse racing should be stopped as it was felt to be a minority sport for the rich. Horse racing was saved due to the influence of Lord Derby representing what he called the 'horse racing industry' and its huge vested interests at the highest government levels.

Attendances at race meetings were, however, very poor, with low levels of gambling and prizes. There were also low attendances at other sporting events. An October 1940 survey in Worcester reported crowds of 2,000 at football and cricket matches that would have attracted 10,000 before the war.

Although county championship matches were cancelled during the 1940 season, the MCC organised a programme of nineteen games: thus giving a lead to those counties that were undecided whether or not to play.

Many clubs carried on as usual with the help of locally billeted members of HM forces and club finances often improved since there were fewer playing expenses but continuing income from social events. Many of these 'socials' were staged to raise money for charities and together with periodical friendly matches for good causes held by every sport brought in the following sums between 1939 and 1943:

▦	Whist, bridge and dancing	£365,478
▦	Billiards and snooker	£ 79,919
▦	Darts and bowls	£ 72,186
▦	Soccer	£ 70,236
▦	Golf	£ 67,000
▦	Greyhound racing	£ 50,561
▦	Boxing	£ 25,183
▦	Cricket	£ 22,996
▦	Rugby	£ 10,580
▦	Athletics	£ 9,319
▦	Cycling	£ 6,365
▦	Swimming	£ 1,758
▦	Hockey	£ 480

These figures seem to support the *Mass Observation Report* conclusion that ordinary people withdrew from participation in outdoor sports and spent more time indulging in games and recreations based in public houses and village halls.

Although club finances often benefited during the war, there were some sacrifices, such as that made by Bolton Cricket Club which allowed its square to be used as a vegetable garden during the 'dig for victory' campaign. Many clubs were obliged to alter their constitutions in order to deal with wartime circumstances, so we find that:

▦ The Warrington Public Parks Bowling League introduced Emergency War Rules, which laid down procedures for dealing with games disrupted by air-raids

▦ The Corinthian Sailing Club in Hammersmith changed the level of quoracy at meetings from 18 to 3

▦ The Tyldesley Swimming Club operated with junior members only despite their lack of voting powers

- The Walsall Cycling Club co-opted committee members in contradiction of its policy and decided that 'all future transactions be in cash since so many members are likely to be conscripted'.

The *Mass Observation Report* featuring Oxford sports clubs in June 1941 concluded that all of them had been hit hard and most activities, especially away matches, had been reduced owing to petrol rationing. A notable exception was the local CTC branch, which was able to maintain its normal level of activity without difficulty. The Cheltenham Cycling Club reported with typical English understatement that it was 'in a good position considering the troublesome year we have had'.

Rugby also managed to continue despite talk of a shut down, with *The Daily Mail* of October 23rd, 1939 reporting that 'it will surprise clubs and players to know that the watchful eye of the Rugby Union is still upon them and that even Rugby 13 in the north is carrying on, determined to keep the fans cheerful'.

Lessons learned

One outcome of Britain's involvement in wars abroad was an increasing awareness that the country's international stature was dwindling and that its strategic role was being usurped by the United States of America.

As we have seen, there was a public school tendency to equate military conflict with sporting competition and to judge the nation's strength by its sporting success. Defeats by foreigners at cricket and rowing, together with evidence of poor physical standards amongst the general population, prompted some to identify a creeping moral decline in English society.

The London Olympic Games of 1908 had left many English sportsmen feeling decidedly ambivalent about international competition. The failure of the British Empire to beat the medal tally of the United States team at the Stockholm Olympics in 1912 had allowed critics to conclude that its 'performance has prejudiced our position in the eyes of other people and provoked not a little patronising talk of England's decadence'. Shortly after World War I when Britain's pre-eminence in the world began to be questioned, a total withdrawal from all international sporting competition was contemplated.

The Amateur Rowing Association had concluded in 1923 that 'organised international athletic activity is contrary to the true spirit of amateur sport and endangers friendly relations'.

The following year *The Times* (July 22nd, 1924) endorsed this approach by stating bluntly that 'the Olympic Games is a cause of ill will. Nothing but ill will has been generated at the Paris Olympics' and that in the interests of good international relations there should be 'no more Olympic Games'.

However, in this, as in other things, the sporting establishment and governing bodies were out of step with sportsmen themselves who relished the prospect of stronger competition and argued persuasively to be given a chance to emulate the levels of performance of foreign competitors.

Four years later, attitudes began to change and *The Times* (August 7th, 1928) endorsed the Olympics of 1928 as being 'more satisfactory than any which have

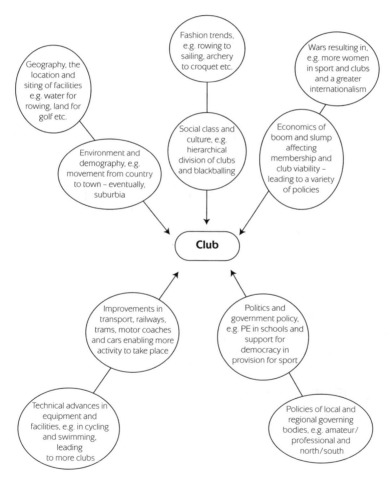

FIGURE 7.1 Influences affecting club fortunes

preceded them' because 'the success of our athletes in the track events should dispose once and for all of the undignified inferiority complex suffered when Britons are beaten'.

Finally, in 1939, even the rowing establishment in the form of the stewards of Henley Royal Regatta, was embracing internationalism in offering to help foreign crews with their travelling expenses, since 'foreign competition is of such great value to English rowing'.

Post-war English sport has been dominated by three major themes:

- increasing internationalism
- government sponsored democratisation
- business induced commercialism.

and we will look at all of these in the next chapter.

QUESTIONS

CLUB FORTUNES

1 Legislation gave working people free time on Saturday afternoons. Why was this not enough?

2 Why did the growth of sport in the middle classes produce more clubs and members whilst in the working classes it produced more spectators?

3 Why was cycling overtaken by boating, tennis and rambling as 'fashionable' activities?

4 Why were some sports considered 'noble, manly and patriotic'?

5 Explain the differing attitudes to sport during the two World Wars.

6 'We need to become more professional in order to remain amateur' – what was meant by this in the context of international sport in England in the early twentieth century.

Suggested further reading

Lowerson, J. and Myerscough, G., *Time to Spare in Victorian England* (Harvester Press, 1977)

Mangan, J.A. and Park, B., *From Fair Sex to Feminism* (Frank Cass, 1992)

Yeo, E. and Yeo, S., *Popular Culture and Class Conflict* (Harvester Press, 1981)

chapter eight

POST-WAR DEVELOPMENTS

An early opportunity should be taken to apply for admittance to the association of unions dealing with entertainment, broadcasting and television.
(Minutes of the Professional Footballers' Union, October 23rd, 1955)

In October 1945, immediately following World War II, Britain was asked if it could host the first Olympic Games to be held for twelve years.

Despite their makeshift character and the exclusion of teams from Germany and Japan, the 1948 London games attracted 6,000 competitors from fifty-nine countries whose exploits were watched by capacity crowds of 80,000 at Wembley stadium and for the first time by over half a million television viewers.

The British came away with three gold medals in the gentlemanly sports of rowing and yachting, helped no doubt by 'the charm and domesticity of Henley where the family atmosphere was absorbed by crews from abroad'. This, together with the unusual distance and nature of the course may very well have given the home crews a distinct advantage.

Lack of success on the track, however, was once again put down to the British disinclination to prepare professionally for the higher levels of international sport and the secretary of the AAA promised a much better showing at the 1952 event.

The war, national service and rationing had all played their part in explanations of Britain's continuing lack of international sporting success and the new Labour government certainly had different priorities – notably welfarism, housing and education – with sport only officially considered as an educational issue.

Changing times

Another legacy of the war was the general recognition that sport was just as likely to boost morale in the peacetime struggle for national prosperity as it had in the wartime battle for national survival. In both war and peace the communal pleasures of sport complemented communal work in factories and football particularly exemplified the growth of sporting spectatorism as a manifestation of social solidarity.

It should be no surprise that attendances at football matches peaked in the late 1940s but have been on a downward trend ever since as increasing prosperity has eroded social and cultural affiliations.

Another example is greyhound racing, which became the second biggest spectator sport after football. Having officially begun in the summer of the General Strike (1926) at Belle Vue in Manchester, it grew quickly to the point where crowds of 25,000 at venues like Hackney stadium were not uncommon, with other big meetings held at the White City stadium, Haringey, Owlerton (Sheffield) and of course at Belle Vue. There were also scores of small rural meetings around the country.

Greyhound racing is currently promoted as a family experience. One of the results of the 1994 amendment to the Sunday Observation Act of 1780 has been the development of 'family afternoons' on Sundays at greyhound tracks in Hove, Canterbury, Wembley and Peterborough.

At the lower socio-economic levels, such solidarity was also evident in rugby league, which maintained and strengthened its hold on the public imagination in Yorkshire and Lancashire. At the upper levels, cricket, horse racing, rowing, golf and rugby union entered a period of slow but steady democratisation.

Staunch, fashionable and genteel support continued for events like the Eton and Harrow cricket match, which was re-established in 1946 on such austere lines that Etonians lacked their bowler hats and the Harrovians their boaters. At the same time there began a gradual breakdown of social hierarchy in the sport, which culminated in 1963 when the distinction between 'gentlemen' and 'players' was finally abolished. Arguably, a more significant milestone in the history of the sport for both players and spectators was the introduction of foreign players into county cricket in 1968.

Financial imperatives required that horse racing was made available to a wider cross section of the public and determined attempts were made to do so. Efforts were made to make race-going less exclusive and gradually admission to members' enclosures was made more accessible and grandstand prices slightly reduced.

Despite a loss of confidence in the administration of the sport, brought about by a series of doping scandals in the 1950s, its future as a popular attraction was assured by the injection of further capital through the Betting Levy Bill in 1960. This allowed the new Levy Board to collect contributions from bookmakers and the tote.

Rowing too...

In rowing, the seeds of social change had been sown in 1890 when the National Amateur Rowing Association (NARA) was established for working men as an alternative to the gentlemen's Amateur Rowing Association (ARA). Following World War II the ARA became increasingly aware that foreign competition had not only caught but also easily surpassed the English crews formed entirely of Oxbridge gentlemen. It thus became necessary to widen the recruitment of oarsmen for international selection and with this end in view the two organisations amalgamated in 1956.

Two sports which proved less receptive to post-war democratisation were golf and rugby union. The former continued to discriminate on grounds of class, gender, religion and occupation, whilst the latter restricted itself (at least ostensibly) to considerations of social class and occupation; stipulating ironically that only 'professional people' were acceptable.

A television personality of the day, Ludovic Kennedy, mentions in his biography, *On My Way to the Club*, that he had been 'blackballed' by his golf club because of his well-known opinions and criticisms of the legal system which allowed so many miscarriages of justice. Club administrators also discriminated against Jews to the extent that the Association of Jewish Golf Clubs and Societies was established to attempt to rectify the situation. Black people were also 'persona non grata'.

The Professional Golf Association (PGA) records that in 1997 there were 3,400 golf professionals and retired members in the UK, of whom *two* were black – Jim Howard at Pontypool GC and Roland West at Altrincham Municipal GC.

And even golf...

During the l980s particularly, the social make-up of golf clubs changed considerably, many being affected not only by the commercial necessity of a wider membership but also by the activities of the Equal Opportunities Commission. The Northwood Golf Club in Middlesex exemplifies this national trend – albeit later than many others – in accepting as members all those applicants capable of paying its subscriptions, although several classes of membership continue to exist. As in many other cases, this club concluded that an 'open door policy' was 'a change for the worse' embarked upon simply out of financial necessity.

Along with others, Northwood allowed its female members neither to vote nor sit on any committee – as well as restricting their playing time to benefit the male members.

From the 1950s the game of rugby union struggled with the paying of expenses to ostensibly amateur players and with a strained relationship with rugby league football. After decades of criticising the Rugby League for paying players, the RFU sanctioned 'legitimate expenses' for those players who were 'in the early stages of a profession'; perhaps forgetting that it was these same legitimate expenses it had denied to working players eighty years earlier.

There are of course cultural divisions even within the rugby union club structure, particularly when rural clubs like Bath play Harlequins from London. Such games reveal an intriguing subtext of regional and class rivalries:

- town versus country
- London versus the provinces
- property developers versus farmers
- public school versus state school
- playing to win versus playing for fun.

Peter Yarranton, a lifelong supporter of Wasps RUFC, lamented the passing of the 'golden days' when the top clubs played each other in a network of contests stretching back through schools and universities but realised that the sport had to become as professional as possible so that the game could remain amateur. He wasn't to know that the new professional attitude to playing would see full-time professionals within a few years of his remarks.

With regard to rugby league, the International Rugby Board (IRB) endorsed a 'Free Gangway' agreement in 1986 that allowed players to be members of both the Amateur Rugby League and Union. In January 1995 the first meeting in 100 years took place between the presidents of the two codes in order to agree ways of making this agreement work in practice.

Women break down barriers

The position of women in sport improved gradually and grudgingly during the post-war period and is only now approaching anything like parity with men.

As we have seen, women in golf are often treated as second-class citizens and further examples of this are to be found in the constitutions of most golf clubs which state that 'lady members shall not be eligible to take part in any management of the club or to act as officers' – even though they often represent a significant proportion of the membership.

The Equal Opportunities Commission was set up in 1975 as a result of the Sex Discrimination Act of that year but the position of women in sports clubs is outside its legal remit. Joanna Foster, a past director of the Commission, has said that 'discriminatory rules within mixed sports clubs are a source of constant complaint to the Commission'. It should be mentioned here that there *are* Ladies' clubs whose male members are not allowed to vote; for example, the Wirral Ladies' Golf Club (1894).

Despite the sexual equality of the war years, much sporting culture reverted to pre-war custom so that even in clubs where women could gain access it was unlikely that they would be treated civilly. Darlington Billiard Club, in its 'new' rules of 1947, prevented members from even buying a drink for a lady.

Most older sports were considered to be male territory and most women were content with that. However, the more recent activities of archery, cycling, tennis and swimming became equally accessible and club membership often shows a predominance of women.

Interestingly, two of the most male-dominated clubs, the MCC and Leander (rowing), which had both resisted the inclusion of women for around two centuries, allowed them across the threshold in the year 2000 since they would otherwise have failed to receive huge grants from the national lottery. Such grants were conditional upon these clubs exercising an 'open-door' policy. This requirement has actually been in force since 1965 when the Sports Development Council was formed.

It is no coincidence that club constitutions everywhere have been changed and that discrimination against women has markedly declined since then. Sixty-five per cent of the clubs surveyed during the writing of this book have received grants from the Sports Council or lottery money through Sport England.

Even an extremely traditional club like the Manchester Wheelers Cycling Club (1890), which specialised in competitive cycling, was encouraged to admit females in 1969 – despite grave misgivings from the older members.

Perhaps the older cyclists knew something? Witness an item in *The Graphic* of the July 13th, 1895 (around the time when many cycling clubs were first established) which was titled 'The Newest Woman – Forward but not Past' and went on:

> **A certain lady cyclist in the suburb of Finchley, riding on the wrong side of the road, ran into another lady and using language, knocked her down, pulled her hair and dragged her across the road. The wearing of rational dress does not apparently make the wearer rational.**

Unlike hunting, horse racing remained male dominated until the mid-1960s when Florence Nagel became the first woman to be granted a training licence, to be followed in 1975 by the first woman professional jockey and in 1977 by the first female member of the Jockey Club.

More recently women have begun to encroach on the bastions of rugby and football, having already established themselves in most other sports either in association with the original governing bodies or through separate organisations. Cricket and hockey have separate governing bodies for women, since the men felt unable to 'officially recognise the existence of the new organisations' when they were formed back in Victorian and Edwardian times. The following sports are today 'unisex' in terms of their administration:

- archery
- basketball
- bowling
- cycling
- rowing
- rugby league
- swimming
- lawn tennis.

The RFU and the FA finally recognised the growth of female participation in their sports in 1994 by granting associate status to the women's governing bodies.

Despite their acceptance by the majority of contact sports, women continue to be denied access to boxing by the Amateur Boxing Association (ABA) but in 1994, some enthusiasts established a Women's Professional Boxing Association and women's bouts are attracting considerable spectator interest in the London area.

Women and post-war sport

The degree to which women generally took up sport in the post-war period continued to give cause for concern to the Sports Council, whose research department repeatedly produced figures that showed as few as 15 per cent of women taking part in any sport on a regular basis. Several initiatives were subsequently implemented with moderate success but further strategies were launched in 1993. Fourteen years later the position has definitely improved and women have achieved parity with men in rowing, bowling and tennis and are 'over-represented' in swimming and aerobics.

The proportion of all adults now taking part in some form of sporting activity on a regular basis has risen above 50 per cent for the first time since 1965 when statistics were first taken.

Making it pay

Along with the process of democratisation it was necessary for those involved in sport to treat their activities more seriously than before in order to survive the post-war period. A football strike in November 1945 for better wages and conditions met with resistance from chairmen who pleaded that an entertainment tax of 40 per cent made it impossible. They finally agreed to a maximum wage of £9 a week, bonus schemes and an injury compensation settlement.

In amateur sport all clubs were forced to re-assess their position in the light of greatly changed circumstances. In cycling the Catford CC managed its post-war debt by trimming its affiliations to governing bodies and by forming a subsidiary company to manage the Herne Hill track in conjunction with the National Cycling Union (NCU). Poorly attended Saturday afternoon track meetings were abandoned and the club joined forces with other clubs to form the London Cyclists' Defence Association. The aim here was to protect cyclists against further restrictions of their liberties and rights on the road as cars became more common.

A tightening up of administration became commonplace in the sport and the Bristol CTC drastically cut the size of its committee and delegated much of its business to regional and national bodies. The Cestreham CC started a 'black book' in 1950, to deter inappropriate behaviour amongst members, with a further threat of suspension from all competitive events.

Renewal of club activities, sometimes after a long wartime lay-off, placed strains on administration and some clubs, like the Portsmouth Corinthian Yacht Club in 1946, were compelled to employ professional secretaries for the first time and to seek mergers with other clubs. Portsmouth merged with the Royal Anglian Yacht Club.

New wage rates affected many clubs as groundsmen and instructors expected to receive improved post-war remuneration. The cost of petrol for away fixtures also proved to be a burden.

Before the war, groundsmen had charged £4 per season but wanted £10 immediately afterwards, while swimming instruction averaged £10 for a pre-war season but £16 afterwards.

New, higher insurance rates made life very difficult for the smaller clubs, some of whom were forced to rent out their fields out of season in order to pay higher insurance premiums.

Inevitably many clubs found the transition to a more businesslike post-war climate impossible. Archery suffered a substantial decline that was only halted during the 1950s with the establishment of county archery associations. The dearth of archery clubs was the subject of an article in *The Times* in July 1948, when there were only six clubs left in the whole of the north west of England.

The new county associations were extremely successful at promoting the sport and by 1990 there were seventy-one clubs well established in the region. This revival was also replicated in other areas.

Many small clubs decided that closer co-operation with a neighbour was the only option open to them and this was very common in the post-war period.

The 'business of sport'

During the 1960s, similar financial imperatives encouraged the growth of a commercial attitude towards sporting activity even at amateur and recreational levels. Club committees were required to consider the provision of social facilities for players and spectators alike and the sponsorship potential for their sport.

It was during this period that breweries invested millions in clubs up and down the country, with Tetley and Whitbread chief amongst them. It was also at this time that the ubiquitous 'fruit machine' first made its appearance as an important source of income for beleaguered club treasurers.

New licensing restrictions required many club constitutions to be amended to include reference to the provision of recreational and other social facilities including the supply of alcoholic refreshments.

Awareness that sponsorship, even at the most basic level, required some public profile for the club saw the encouragement of more supporters onto the touchline and into the bar after the game. Spectator appeal became almost as important for amateur sport as it had always been for the professionals.

After 1965 higher levels of fund-raising were attempted by the amateur sector in order to maximise the 'pound for pound' grant-aid available from the Sports Council. Many clubs also began to experience vandalism and funds were desperately needed to repair and renew premises.

Not everyone welcomed the new commercial initiatives and the amateur dilemma was based on whether to change the way things were run in order to attract wider interest and/or funding or respect the traditional ways of doing things and risk being left behind.

Recreation versus 'win-at-all-costs'

It was for the preservation of just this 'character' that most amateur clubs continued to strive in the face of growing commercialism and a professionalism born of higher competitive standards. This trend away from 'amateur' behaviour was causing worries elsewhere.

Some concerns were reflected in a remark made at a conference concerning physical education and its future in boarding schools, held at Marlborough College in 1970: 'As schoolteachers one of our greatest enemies may be the increasing expertise of win-at-all-costs professionalism'.

There were, however, some clubs that turned to commercialism simply to survive. The huge growth in sponsored rowing events during the 1970s and 1980s owed more to the instinct of self-preservation in a sport where clubs are dependent on the success of one or two annual regattas than to any planned development policy. Some regattas have reverted to an eighteenth-century level of commercialism, employing fairground attractions to subsidise the rowing events: e.g. Burton-on-Trent, Whitby and Putney Town.

In sports involved in league-style competitions, the pressure for success has led to previously unheard of levels of business activity. In 1980 the Durham Cricket Club recognised that its accounts 'needed a great deal of hard work'. Keen to maintain its position as one of the country's foremost clubs it amended its constitution to allow the appointment of a chairman who could revitalise the club by securing commercial sponsorship. Similar activity was being repeated throughout the premier leagues.

Whilst leagues had been part of cricket for 100 years, in the 1980s they were very new in rugby union and were introduced with a view to encouraging much needed spectator, commercial and media interest at a time when rugby league was reaping the benefits of substantial television coverage.

The traditional fixtures network of rugby union clubs was largely destroyed by the new league system which led inevitably to a professionalisation of the sport as the larger clubs established trust funds to recruit and retain the best players.

Violence, indiscipline and declining standards of sportsmanship

One worrying result of fiercer competition has been an increase in the level of on-field violence. This has been explained by:

- the pressure exerted by media scrutiny
- the obsession with winning as a result of the greater availability of large prizes
- the failure of governing bodies to develop an adequate framework of regulation and control.

During the 1990s it became fashionable to link the decline in sporting standards with a general collapse of values in society as a whole. Of course this has happened regularly over the centuries, beginning as early as the fourteenth century, shown in society's intolerance of football and the other unlawful sports.

Nevertheless, the increasing violence in sport became headline news in the early 1990s and it was felt that governing bodies were doing little to bring players into line. The Central Council for Physical Recreation (CCPR) established an arbitration panel in 1993, designed to deal with contentious issues in any sport.

Two particular examples of sporting violence led to the formation of the above panel; one being the severe head injury suffered by Gary Mabbutt, then captain of Tottenham Hotspur FC, and the other being the death of Seamus Lavelle, the Hendon RFC player, whose manslaughter by a fellow player resulted in a six-month prison sentence.

Nigel Hook of the CCPR told the inquiry into Lavelle's death: 'the rules of sport should primarily govern the behaviour of the players, not the law of the land. In an ideal world there is no place for sport in the courts since it is an affair between two consenting adults'.

Greater professionalism and the need to regulate the sport more closely led to the Rugby Union finally accepting the inevitable and the sport became 'open' with the payment of wages becoming the norm.

Money from television coverage and all the associated media opportunities was the spur for the bigger clubs to organise themselves into a league system and so, eventually, that bastion of Corinthian amateurism the RFU was forced to recognise the financial imperatives of modern sport.

In 1922, when the Rugby League was established, the gentlemen of the Rugby Union criticised it for capitulating to 'the curse of gate money' and yet – eighty-five years later – it capitulated to what we now might call 'the curse of television money'.

The media millions

Commercial activity in professional sport continued to grow during the post-war period, so that by the 1980s it had become big business in England and a huge industry worldwide. Responsibility for this lies largely with the financial appeal of television, which first made itself felt at the Wimbledon Lawn Tennis Championships of 1937 when a few hundred Londoners viewed twenty-five minutes of a men's singles match.

By the early 1970s, fees from television were providing 20 per cent of the total income for the championships. By 1987, at £9 million, this had grown to 60 per cent and today it is 80 per cent – thanks to the hard work of the television marketing executive and his team employed by the Wimbledon club.

Wimbledon's television executive was first recruited in 1993 when television contracts were due for renegotiation. The job advert mentioned that 'since television coverage has increased dramatically in recent years a senior executive is needed to market and manage these contracts worldwide'.

Well aware of the power of media exposure, the Professional Footballers' Association (PFA) established a sub-committee in 1955 to explore its potential with the advice to itself that 'we should take a firm stand on the question of Broadcasting and Television or be guilty of dereliction of duty to our members'. The sub-committee realised that clubs would make a lot of money from the media and that little or none of it would be shared with the players who provided the entertainment.

At the same time club chairmen feared that the growth of media coverage was likely to reduce match attendances. They may well have been right since over the long term, there does seem to have been a decline in attendances at football matches. This gave valuable ammunition to those who promoted and established a premier division in order to consolidate attendances for the best clubs and maximise television income.

Average First Division football attendances dropped from 28,704 in the 1970s to 18,766 in the 1980s and to 18,273 in the 1990s.

Evidence strongly suggests that the success of this premier division has disadvantaged all the clubs in lower divisions. Derek Dougan, Chairman of the PFA in the early 1970s, was largely responsible for extending the commercial profile of the game with a view to maximising his members' income. He believed that 'we should sell it the best way we can'.

The English game was not quite ready for Dougan's commercial vision so he went to the USA to help with the growth of the game where they better understand product management. In fact the commercial potential of the game has only recently become obvious with the growth of satellite TV and the global markets it has opened for those clubs big enough to exploit it.

Television takes over...

Football continued to exemplify the Thatcherite revolution, where local club chairmen were replaced by thrusting entrepreneurs who knew (or thought they knew) how to market the game. This free-market approach saw top clubs creaming off most of the television revenue whilst poorer clubs found it more difficult to make ends meet – despite promises that prosperity would eventually trickle down to them.

The original agreement with the BSkyB television company in 1993 guaranteed the Premier Division clubs £1.5 million per year each for five years. In agreeing this contract the company forced those unwilling or unable to pay for the sports channel to do without television coverage. The failure of prosperity to trickle down to the lower clubs also suggests that the system needs adapting since the domination of a few successful clubs is likely to neuter the appeal of professional sport, which thrives on the uncertainty of the result.

In 1995 there was serious suggestion of a second Premier Division to include some of the First Division clubs and allow them a slice of the television cake. Naturally, the Premier Division chairmen vetoed any such idea as it would inevitably reduce the size of their own slices of the cake.

Early regional television coverage of rugby league encouraged its governing body to solicit commercial sponsorship during the 1970s and this was so successful that by the 1980s it had become the most important element in the game. Almost unnoticed, television became essential as sponsors took advantage of an association with a sport so much in the public eye – at least in the north of England.

The reduction of the game's top division into a super league of fourteen clubs in 1996 was calculated to encourage greater commercial support and this proved successful when it was announced that the sport's three main competitions would yield £5 million in sponsorship.

Similar television coverage of the one-day 'knock-out' competitions in cricket introduced the idea of brand marketing, advertising and sponsorship to a game which had become almost moribund during the 1960s.

The Test and County Cricket Board was responsible, along with the newly formed Cricket Council, for encouraging television coverage of county games and of Test cricket. The income from these contracts was used to promote the game nationally; partly by funding development officers to introduce a new generation to the joys of playing cricket.

Individual county clubs have begun to use their facilities for overtly commercial purposes whenever possible, often using pavilion extensions or marquees to cater for the conference market. At the same time sponsors for teams and individual players, many of which are breweries, have been secured for every competition large or small.

The growth of financial support for professional sport over recent decades has undoubtedly influenced the perception of commercialism in the amateur sector. As early as the 1950s Horst Dassler was handing out free shoes to athletes at the Melbourne Olympics, a practice that enabled Adidas to dominate the industry for the next 25 years.

Sponsorship from companies such as Prudential Assurance and Trustee Savings Bank together with television contracts have turned even club athletics into a lucrative business. Before professionalism proper a successful athlete was required to pay any winnings or commercial endorsements into a personal trust fund; none of which could be touched until his or her retirement from athletics.

Today the sport is 'open' and athletes are paid what the entertainment market thinks they are worth.

Paula Radcliffe, the world marathon record holder, became a millionaire when she won the 2002 Chicago marathon in a world record time. Top sports performers are paid 'appearance money' by promoters who use them to attract spectators and television contracts – and in turn commercial sponsors. Paula will now be paid a substantial appearance fee wherever she runs because, as David Moorcroft of UK Athletics says, 'she's a girl who can fill a stadium just by agreeing to be there'.

In order to increase media appeal, a four-yearly World Track and Field Championships was introduced in 1983, which was so commercially successful that it became a biennial event in 1993. Similar inducements have seen the creation of a World Cup in Rugby Union and the introduction of league competition, which resulted in television coverage of club matches and sponsorship worth £7 million from Courage Brewers.

In other sports the same commercial imperative is at work. Most golf clubs now rely heavily on the proceeds from the professional's shop, catering and bar profits and income from gaming machines, which began in the 1960s and 1970s.

The accounts of Warrington Golf Club for 1978 show that income included:

■ sponsorship   £5,000

■ the bar   £23,000

■ gaming machines   £7,000
                    ─────────
                    £35,000

This sum dwarfed the income from members' subscriptions but even this level of income could not prevent the club losing £2,300 over the year.

Even cycling clubs have derived commercial benefits from increased television coverage of the sport during the 1980s and 1990s. A good example of the commercial 'fall out' from television coverage is provided by the Manchester Wheelers' Cycling Club, which suffered a significant post-war decline but was rescued by sponsorship from Trumann's Steel. This enabled the club to recruit some of the leading riders of the day who added significantly to its long list of achievements. Some of these riders, such as Steve Joughin, Malcolm Elliot and Daryl Webster, went on to successful professional careers.

In rowing, that most Corinthian of sports, commercialism began in 1985 with television broadcasts of the Leyland Daf Challenge Sprints. Those twin champions of the amateur ethic, the Oxford and Cambridge University Boat Clubs, now have fully professional staffs paid for out of the £400,000 that they each receive every season from television contracts and sponsorship.

Sport or just 'business'?

Commercialism has professionalised much former amateur activity and at the same time redefined professional sport as a business. Those sports that were professionalised in order to provide participants with much needed additional income have now become extremely specialised, to the extent that they exclude everyone except the most talented, who will have emerged only after years of grooming, training, sponsorship support and personal promotion by some form of institutional management.

The sport of professional boxing, for example, only attained official status with the establishment of the British Boxing Board of Control in 1929 – at a time when an economic depression drove the unemployed to try their fists at prize-fighting. For centuries before, and for half a century afterwards, men had dabbled with the sport semi-professionally at a range of venues. One of these venues was the fairground boxing-booth, of which there were around 100 in the post-war period. Here, around 1,000 fighters registered with the British Boxing Board found part-time employment.

The Excelsior Pavilion was a booth run by Ron Taylor which had been in his family since 1843. Like many others it was valued for providing as much ring experience in one month as a training gymnasium might in three. As the registered number of boxers diminished during the 1950s and 1960s, the booths slowly went out of business with the Excelsior reckoned to be the last when it too closed for business in 1994. The same year saw the formation of the Professional Boxing Association (PBA).

The PBA was established to set new professional standards for its 350 members and Barry McGuigan, its president, said at the first annual meeting that 'our sport has for too long had too many seedy connotations with the boxers themselves being the least consideration of all'.

Once again television has created a commercial business from a sporting activity, with the result that the journeyman professional has been largely replaced by expertly managed super athletes whose success depends almost as much on their media profile and personality as their boxing skills.

The effect of television on boxing can be seen in the proliferation of manufactured 'championships' that draw large TV audiences and attract big sponsorship. Originally there had been only one champion for each weight classification;

now there are three new international governing bodies and several new weight classifications, all designed to increase the number of championship bouts and therefore television income.

In football, as in boxing, the immediate post-war period also saw a growth in numbers with a record 2,714 professionals affiliated to the Players' Union in 1949. The union renamed itself the Professional Footballers' Association (PFA) in 1958 – largely as a public relations exercise – and immediately gained representation on the FA Council.

Negotiations between the FA, the PFA and the Football League eventually resulted in the abolition of the maximum wage of £15 per week for First Division players, which was close to average earnings at that time. Club owners, however, held on to the 'retain and transfer' system of players' registration (and thereby employment) which denied players any independence.

This matter came to a head in 1963 when George Eastham of Newcastle United wished to move to Arsenal but was prevented from doing so by the Newcastle board of directors. This was successfully contested by Eastham in the courts – with the backing of the PFA.

In the George Eastham case in 1963, Lord Justice Wilberforce found that 'the old retain and transfer system was an employers system set up in an industry where the employers have established a monolithic front where they are more strongly organised than the employees and represents an unjustifiable restraint of trade'.

From then onwards and with increasing rapidity following the growth of television coverage, the importance of individual players grew to the point where they have become (along with their agents) dominant factors in the football industry. This has unearthed many compromising situations with regard to transfer fees, perhaps the best known being that involving George Graham who, as manager of Arsenal FC, was alleged to have received £285,000 from an agent to employ his client, which – it was also alleged – he then did. Graham was dismissed from Arsenal FC on February 21st, 1995.

The rise and rise of the agent

The representation of professional sportsmen was already big business in golf. Mark McCormack's International Management Group began by developing the career of Arnold Palmer, including his promotion of the Open Championship in England from 1960 onwards.

For most of the previous century golf in England had been overwhelmingly amateur and middle class but wealthier clubs had long employed golf 'professors' as coaches and trainers. These professors always augmented their wages with prizes from professional tournaments, often sponsored by the popular newspapers of the day.

Limited television coverage began during the 1950s and following the Centenary Open Championship in 1960 there grew up a class of tournament professional whose income derived exclusively from prize monies and commercial endorsements.

As more players joined the tournament 'circus', attracted by ever-greater financial inducements, it was found that the existing number of events was no longer adequate. In 1976, the Professional Golfers' Association (PGA) established the European Tour, which provided players and sponsors alike with greater commercial opportunities. By this time the best English professionals were travelling the globe seeking the most lucrative events, so that once again commercial pressures have resulted in a standard of play that can only be attained by those few who monopolise the major championships and prize funds. Currently, this 'few' is actually only one – Tiger Woods – who receives $1 million as 'appearance money'.

Commercial pressures also forced the inclusion of professionals in the Wimbledon Championships in 1968 and this led directly to the abolition of the distinction between amateurs and professionals by the International Tennis Federation. It was the beginning of the 'open' era and a rare modern-day example of England setting an international trend.

The rise of commercialism in tennis has resulted in huge prize funds, a proliferation of tournaments and – as in other sports – the emergence of a few 'star' players who play far too much tennis. Boris Becker maintained that in his day all of the top players 'were badly injured or having a nervous breakdown' which is why players today travel with their own coaches, physiotherapists and sports psychologists.

'Open' competition has necessarily blurred the distinction between amateur and professional to the point where it has become irrelevant. The most Corinthian of sports now accept that some form of payment is reasonable and even the IOC dropped the word 'amateur' from its charter as far back as 1972.

Such prestige is now attached to winning Olympic gold medals that the competition has been called a 'war without weapons'; helped by the Olympic oath which speaks of 'honour of country and the glory of sport' and not the other way around. When the commercial pressures exerted by global sponsorship are added to this the result is a potent mix of vested interests, some of which are mutually exclusive.

TABLE 8.1 The post-war growth of commercialism, democracy and participation, and internationalism

Commercialism	Democracy and participation	Internationalism
Sports become businesslike due to economic necessity	Government places greater emphasis on school sport	Foreign teams beat us
Greater 'spectatorism' as reaction to wartime restrictions	Sports club and governing body amalgamations make sport less exclusive	Sports hire professional coaches for the first time
First mass TV coverage of sport on BBC 'Grandstand'	Sports Development Council established in 1965; 'Sport for All' becomes national policy	Governing bodies affiliate to international organisations
Maximum wages abolished as a 'restraint of trade'	Amateur/professional divide eroded by a range of payments	Foreign players begin to play for English clubs
The beginning of 'open' competition	Women progress with Sex Discrimination Act (1975) and participation increases	Sports begin to hire foreign coaches
Unions, agents and managements companies promote players	'Open' competition, due to commercial pressures	Sports Aid Foundation and business sponsorship fund medal prospects
Government encourages business sponsorship of sport	Regular participation in sport rises to over 50% of the population for the first time (2000)	English governing bodies host and organise World Championships
Growth of competitions and 'championships' in order to supply TV demand	Inter-school fixtures fell by 70% between 1995 and 2005	Most sports have now won European or World Championships
TV marketing executives hired by sports bodies	Government has increased funding for sport by 28% between 2000 and 2007	11 gold medals at Sydney Olympics (2000)
Emergence of 'superstars' and appearance money to promote events		9 gold medals at Athens Olympics (2004)
Global satellite TV sport – 24 hours a day, turnover in billions of pounds.		

The change in the English attitude to Olympic sport is reflected in the fact that the British Olympic Association (BOA) now utilises the services of a Competitors' Employment Officer to find jobs for sportsmen and women 'whose careers are affected by the heavy demands of their training schedules'. Performers identified as medal prospects also receive substantial financial support from the Sports Aid Foundation and are also likely to receive commercial sponsorship.

The income of individuals such as Sir Steven Redgrave, the five times Olympic gold medal winner, has rarely dropped below £50,000 for the last ten years and in his case such a sum might now be commanded for appearing at an event.

The poor showing of the British athletic team at the London Olympics of 1948 encouraged the Amateur Athletic Association to employ professional coaches for the first time and establish a national coaching infrastructure. Despite this, Chris Brasher's gold medal in the steeplechase in 1956 was Britain's first individual gold medal in track athletics since 1932. Only relatively recently has substantial commercial sponsorship enabled athletes to attain and maintain the degree of fitness necessary to compete successfully at the highest level.

British success in the commercialised post-war world of international sport has been a long time in coming. It was not until well after the war that the implications of specialisation funded by commercialism in the West and massive state subsidy in the East was fully realised as being the key to élite sporting performances.

Once this became apparent the transition from well meaning amateurism to polished professionalism took a generation to achieve.

Is British best?

International competition demonstrated just how far English sport and its administrators had fallen behind the rest of the world. However, using this as motivation, most, if not all, our major sports have since produced European or World champions. Below is a list of sports with the country that first showed up our competitive weakness:

- Athletics – Russia
- Cycling – France
- Football – Hungary
- Golf – USA
- Hockey – Pakistan

- Rowing – Germany
- Rugby – New Zealand
- Swimming – Australia.

Boxing and bowling have maintained their traditional success whilst cricket and tennis have simply failed to embrace the new competitive ethic. It would seem that post-war developments domestically have shown sport responding to a variety of societal forces. In doing so domestic sport has developed a commercialism and professionalism ideally suited to the new entrepreneurial age. It has in fact become a new industry.

QUESTIONS

POST-WAR DEVELOPMENTS

1   In what respect was sport an agent of social solidarity in post-war England?

2   How did the abolition of 'gentlemen' and 'players' in cricket reflect social values?

3   How have equal opportunities legislation and the criteria for Sport England grant-aid improved the 'lot' of women in sport?

4   Why is 'league-based' competition a necessary component of televised sport?

5   Has 'TV money' revitalised the game of cricket, or simply glossed over the cracks?

6   Has top-level sport simply become a tool of big business?

Suggested further reading

Holt, R., *Sport and the Working Class in Modern Britain* (Manchester University Press, 1992)

McCrone, K., *Sport and the Physical Emancipation of English Women* (Lutterworth Press, 1988)

Roberts, J., *The Commercial Sector in Leisure* (The Sports Council, 1979)

chapter nine

SPORT AS AN INDUSTRY

Take away sponsorship and commercialism from sport and what have you left? A large sophisticated engine developed over 100 years with no fuel.

(Dick Pound, Vice President, International Olympic Committee, 2005)

Consider the following statistics:

- At the beginning of the third millennium, sport and leisure provides employment for 2.5 million people. This is more than the construction or transport industries

- One in every five new jobs created is in sport and leisure

- Between 1976 and 2006 consumer spending on sport increased by 220 per cent

- Sport-related economic activity was in the region of £13.5 billion in 2006, nearly 2 per cent of the UK gross domestic product.

- The 2012 Olympic Games in London will create 12,000 permanent jobs and add £10 billion to annual construction output. It will generate an extra 2 million visitors to the UK who will spend £5 billion in the leisure market.

These figures tell us that sport is an industry of massive proportions. How is it possible to go from hitting a ball for sheer pleasure to a £13.5 billion industry? If we consider the information contained in earlier chapters we can trace the development of a sporting industry in England through every century:

- the fifteenth-century inn-keeper who kept dice for gambling and balls and skittles
- acrobats and tumblers of the fairs and markets of the sixteenth century
- aristocracy who developed horse racing in the seventeenth century
- commercialisation of sport in the eighteenth century
- professionalisation of sport in the nineteenth century
- influence of television in the twentieth century.

These and other developments chart the progress of sport from 'play' to serious business. What is often overlooked is that a sporting economy consists of more than the gate money of the spectators and the wages of the players. It involves many businesses, which together make an industry, namely:

- construction of sports facilities; stadia, tracks, courts, pools etc.
- design, development and manufacture of sports equipment
- design, development and manufacture of sports shoes and clothing
- advertising and promotion; public notices, press, radio and TV
- sporting press; specialist newspapers, magazines, annuals and directories
- sports merchandising; sells almost anything by association with sport
- betting and gambling; dependent on sport for its existence
- sports sponsorship; has grown with television coverage
- sports management; agents, unions, associations, marketing groups: all sell and promote players/events/sports
- the government; promotes sport as a public good and funds sports through Sport England.

All of which make a significant contribution to that £13.5 billion industry.

Each of these businesses is dependent on the existence of professional sport; although the amateur participant also needs facilities, equipment and clothing. Professional sport continues to be financed by the spectator although the viewing might nowadays be via the television company and its satellite technology. Nevertheless, directly or otherwise, it is still the spectator who pays the players' wages.

Wages and that 'accursed gate-money' have changed considerably over the years. In 1879 the great Dr Grace could be watched for sixpence and in that year he received £1,458 as a testimonial bonus. He received another of £9,073 in 1883 and in 1891 he was paid £3,000 for his tour of Australia. As we have seen, his regular 'wage' was £15 a match; probably several times a week but this was because he was a 'star'.

Ordinary cricketers were paid £5 a match and footballers slightly less. By 1930 footballers had hardly progressed with wages of £4 – around the average weekly working wage of that time; and yet they were bought for considerable sums of around £2,000, which represented about four times the national average income.

The minimum weekly wage for footballers was set at £15 in 1950, which was again about the national average, but by 2001 top players like Roy Keane at Manchester United (the first £100,000 a week player) were earning 200 times the national average. The Manchester club also bought Rio Ferdinand for 800 times the average annual wage in 2001.

Sporting millionaires – but at what cost?

The differential between the incomes of top players and those of the spectators make it difficult for the majority of paying customers to identify with those on the pitch and may help to explain why football attendance has been declining since the late 1940s.

Football is the 'market leader' in both gate-money income and wage expenditure and it may be that the ceiling for wages has been reached at last. Hayden Evans (a football agent) has said that 'the ceiling for wages is determined by the power in soccer' – which is Sky TV's money – and yet, with the collapse of ITV Digital in 2002, it has become apparent that clubs are simply paying too much in wages.

In 1999, the annual report of Deloitte and Touche into the game's finances noted that football was growing at a rate that 'all other businesses would die for'. However, it also warned that unless players' wages were controlled, the future for many clubs would be bleak. There are currently only four or five clubs trading at a profit.

Premier League clubs have a combined income greater than all the other seventy-two Football League clubs, who are individually and collectively, massively in debt. In November 2002, the Football League introduced a salary cap with clubs agreeing to limit wages to 60 per cent, and subsequently 50 per cent of their turnover. Even the 'haves' of the Premier League and G-14, which represents Europe's leading clubs, limited players' wages to 80 per cent of turnover in 2005.

Television has advanced considerably since the first Wimbledon broadcast of 1937 when a lady violinist was ready in the studio just in case the TV picture was lost. The latest innovation is digital television and 'pay per view' where viewers pay to watch a particular event rather than subscribe to a channel. This is the latest way in which the spectator pays the entrance fee; which in turn pays the players' wages. The rise in wages has meant that the entrance fees have been escalating to keep pace.

Price rises between 1996 and 2006 have been:

- athletics   215 per cent
- cricket   208 per cent
- tennis   371 per cent
- golf   195 per cent
- racing   142 per cent
- rugby   200 per cent
- football   210 per cent.

Certainly the gate receipts of football clubs remain the single most important component of revenue. Everton FC has 21,000 season ticket holders and a turnover of £19 million, of which £9 million comes from gate money. This money comes unfortunately from richer, older supporters and the high prices are keeping out the younger ones.

The Football Supporters' Association has said that 'the great thing about football and its strength as the national game was its wide social base but this is now narrowing in both social and age terms'. Football's relative loss of younger spectators may be rugby's gain since both codes are now very well supported by youngsters, often in family groups.

Another major expenditure for football clubs is spending on facilities. Whilst in 1899 Tottenham Hotspur FC raised a share issue of £8,000 to build its first stadium at White Hart Lane, that club today is spending £75 million to refurbish its stadium and extend its seating capacity (originally 2,000) to 70,000. Again a share issue will be raised to cover the cost. Tottenham was the first football club to be quoted on the Stock Exchange in 1983.

Other clubs are planning new stadia, the reason being that Premier League sides are attracting 93 per cent capacity crowds and need bigger grounds.

Nor is football the only sport spending big money on facilities:

- one new rowing course and two planned for the near future
- every county cricket ground has new or improved spectator facilities and all have new conference facilities
- thanks to the 2002 Commonwealth Games, there is a new indoor velodrome in Manchester
- 50 new golf courses built since 2000
- Wimbledon has a new No. 1 court and new extra courts
- every Premier Division rugby union club has improved spectator and social facilities
- 3,000 small capital projects at grass-roots level have been completed since 2000
- a new all-weather horse racing course opened at Great Leighs, Essex in 2004.

The money for such ventures comes from share issues, fund-raising inside the sports, private and business sponsorship, television money and government money augmented with lottery grants.

The new course at Great Leighs has been funded largely by the sport and by private money and is the first new course to break into the racing market since 1927, largely because the conditions laid down by the Jockey Club have been so strict.

However, in 2002 the Office of Fair Trading investigated the British Horseracing Board (the Jockey Club under a new name) and found several problems with the way in which the sport is run including the system of allocating race meetings.

Traditionally, racetracks request fixtures and the British Horseracing Board grants them as it sees fit. The Office of Fair Trading feels that a racecourse is a business and should be allowed to stage a meeting if it feels it can make a profit by doing so.

The Director of e-gaming at Ladbrokes, the biggest betting firm, has said that such freedom would create disorder in the short term but that the market would deal with that – as it always does.

There may be no role for the BHB in such a world and the long tradition of the Jockey Club, which began in 1750 with a meeting of gentlemen at the Star and Garter Inn in London, will be over.

'Going down the gym'

One of the consequences of increased exposure for sport has been a fashionable trend towards personal fitness. Ironically, a simultaneous obsession with food has caused massive obesity problems and has also fuelled an appetite for 'fighting the flab' and getting fit.

In 1987, David Lloyd, an ex-international tennis player, raised enough money to build a fitness centre with tennis facilities at Heston, West London. This was so successful that there are now 2,200 fitness organisations with a total of 2 million members: that is one in ten working adults.

According to Mintel, a market research company, one in three adults would like to join a fitness club. Turnover in this sector of the market is over £1 billion and currently there are seventy-six new clubs being built at a cost of £4 million each. The equipment alone for such clubs costs in the region of £1.2 million.

The technological revolution

The design and manufacture of equipment has been a significant part of the sports industry for well over 150 years and began with the growth of professionalism. One major determinant of the growth of sport was – and remains – technological innovation. Equipment has evolved in line with design and materials over the decades. If we take three quite dissimilar sports we can show that:

- in golf, the original heavy wooden clubs were replaced with lighter, more flexible wood; later still, metal alloys were used and these gave way to a range of plastic materials. Then came carbon fibre, Kevlar and, currently, titanium.

- in cycling, the originals were 'hobby horse' machines made of heavy wood and later iron which were replaced by tubular metal, lighter, higher tensile metals, carbon fibre and now Kevlar.

■ in rowing, boats were heavy, built with overlapping planks and later with lighter, cold-moulded smooth plywoods. There are now new materials: plastic, then carbon fibre and (again) Kevlar.

The common theme of all these advances has been the combination of lightness with strength; and whilst this is most obvious in golf, cycling and rowing, it also applies to many other sports. The balls in practically all bat/ball sports have evolved in this way, as have the bats and rackets that strike them. We now have play that is faster and more accurate, making performances more entertaining for the spectator.

Although detailed figures aren't available it is reasonable to suggest that turnover approaches £3 billion a year. As in so many other areas, sport reflects the rather depressed state of English manufacturing since so little sporting equipment is actually produced in this country.

The Reebok range of 'trainers', referred to in an earlier chapter as Foster's shoes of Bolton in 1900, has become part of an American-owned company with the overwhelming majority of its products being produced in southeast Asia where wage costs are so much lower than in Europe. It has diversified into sports clothing generally and its current annual turnover in the UK market is in the region of £300 million.

If we take into consideration the other major players in the sports clothes market, such as Nike (the market leader for shoes) and Adidas, then this sector contributes another £1 billion to the sports industry.

One of the most potent ways of selling merchandise to the public is to pay a well-known sports 'star' to promote it. In the past, personalities such as W.G. Grace were used and today's best example is David Beckham. The difference between the two lies in their payment. Grace might have received fifty guineas for a magazine product endorsement whilst Beckham's 'image rights' are sold for millions due to the selling power of television.

The sporting press and the media

There have been sporting magazines since the 1880s and particularly popular were those for boxing, football, rugby, cricket, cycling and hockey.

Even 120 years ago sports journalism was a flourishing business. The daily sporting papers such as *The Sportsman*, *The Sporting Chronicle* and *Sporting Life* were selling 300,000 copies per day.

Today there are eight national daily papers with a combined circulation of 12 million copies, 10 per cent of the content of which are to do with sport.

There are also thirty-two monthly magazines covering all the major sports and most of the minor ones, which together have a combined circulation of 1.3 million copies.

In 2002, *The Observer* began to issue a monthly sport supplement because it was clear that there was sufficient advertising potential to make it a profitable venture. Magazine advertising can bring in £1,000 for a full colour page, which is a very attractive proposition for publishers.

If we add to the above list of publications relatively new magazines such as *Sports Industry*, which covers the manufacture and provision of sports facilities, that adds another £300 million to the industry's annual turnover.

TV rules...

Although the written word and accompanying images have their place in the promotion of sport they cannot really compete with television coverage in terms of effectiveness.

The televising of sport began in England in 1937 when few people had TV sets and by 1948 there were half a million viewers. By the 1960s, 83 per cent of households had television and today the figure is 97 per cent: thus giving sponsors and advertisers almost blanket coverage of the population.

The fees charged by television companies (and the BBC for transmission fees) have increased commensurately. The BBC paid £1,000 to televise the 1948 London Olympics but today those same rights sell for £1 billion.

The reason that television companies are so particularly interested in sport is that sport is by far the best medium for catching, building and maintaining an audience – better than films, drama, news, quizzes or even soap operas. This is vital in attracting advertisers who make the real profit for the television companies.

BSkyB in particular has achieved a near monopoly in television rights acquisitions. In 2001 it broadcast 21,000 hours of sport (or 65 per cent of the total) whilst the BBC managed only 1,500 hours (just 5 per cent). Since 1998 Murdoch's market share has risen by 27 per cent whilst the BBC's has fallen by 10 per cent.

In September 2002 Sky television tightened its grip on British football by securing the broadcasting rights to the Champions League for the first time in a deal that will see every game in the tournament shown live. ITV have limited rights to screen some games and with Sky have agreed jointly to pay around £84 million each year until 2006. BSkyB now has exclusive rights to the Premiership, the Football League and the Champions League.

The argument is that television is only interested in élite sport so that its money only goes to the top teams. Those teams then become ever more powerful as is the case with clubs such as Arsenal and Manchester United.

The same has occurred in rugby league which, partly to compete with football, reinvented itself in the 1990s with a new Superleague. Now four clubs, Wigan, St Helens, Leeds and Bradford, dominate the game with most other clubs unable to compete. York's rugby league club went into liquidation in March 2002 and although it has since been resurrected it is unlikely to be the last to suffer such indignity.

In cricket little seems to matter other than the success of the national side. Television rights generate 90 per cent of the sport's income and TV companies will pay more if the England side is winning. County matches, which once drew massive crowds, now attract very few and this may well decline further as television concentrates only on the élite aspects of the sport. It may well be that some counties will go out of business altogether.

Such stories abound in rugby union, tennis and boxing and the future for grass-roots sport may rely on whether television money is redistributed to smaller clubs by the governing bodies of the sports involved.

The massive promotional opportunities offered by television mean that sports sponsorship outstrips that for sectors such as the arts, community projects or heritage.

Sports sponsorship

In 2006, sports sponsorship was worth £530 million, which was five per cent up on 2005. This money was invested because sponsors knew that their chosen sport would have extensive television exposure and their brand image would reach millions of homes. The biggest sponsor in 2006 was Adidas, sponsor of Chelsea FC for £90 million over ten years. The most popular sports for sponsorship are currently (in order):

- football
- Rugby Union
- golf

- cricket

- Rugby League.

In 1985 the Institute for Sports Sponsorship was established to encourage business support for sport and 1992 saw the launch of Sportsmatch. This scheme made grants to grass-roots clubs of £1 for every 'business £' that they could raise. With no television income these clubs have had to raise £55 million in the last ten years, whilst televised sports have raised £4 billion over the same period.

Management groups

With such huge sums of money involved it is not surprising that sport has attracted the interest of agents and management groups. In football there are fifty FIFA-licensed agents in the UK. With sport representing around two per cent of the gross domestic products of the UK, the USA and most of Europe, corporate management is moving in to organise the sports industry.

Mark McCormack's International Management Group has become the biggest sports management and marketing company in the world. It plans to get bigger still by buying the clubs its clients play for and has begun with Strasbourg FC in France. Other groups such as the Marquee Group, the Octagon Group, First Artists and Park Associates all agree that 'the industry is ripe for consolidation because we need to pull all the elements together'.

The bigger the management group, the easier it is to link the three elements which are vital to maximise profits: the 'stars', the media and the sponsors; and if it owns most of these in the first place, so much the better. Sport is a worldwide industry and management groups need a foothold in every country so that, as Alan Pascoe says, 'the money that companies are paying to sponsor events and the TV exposure they're getting means that what happens in China is just as important as what's happening in the States or anywhere else'. It seems inevitable that some management groups will merge to form even bigger businesses in order to secure a position in the global market.

The pay-per-view television revolution will accelerate the process as agencies seek to create sporting events to sell to television – just as Mark McCormack did 30 years ago with the World Match Play Championship at Wentworth in Surrey.

Promoting sport

The elements of sports promotion were previewed in the Palmer Report, commissioned by the CCPR in 1988. It said that organisers of high level sports events could secure finance from a range of sources, including:

- entry fees
- gate money
- commercial sponsorship
- television fees
- programme sales
- merchandising
- corporate hospitality
- marketing deals
- personality promotion.

Merchandise and corporate hospitality are huge earners for sport. It is football that dominates this sector of the market although other sports make significant contributions.

The merchandising activities of one club, Chelsea FC, illustrate how money comes in via:

- the club shop
- other retail outlets at home and abroad
- catalogue sales.

Products include mountain bikes, duvet covers, curtains, watches, dressing gowns, videos, bedside lamps, bags, casual shirts and the club's replica kit with everything carrying its logo.

For this and a few other Premiership clubs, the business earns around £100 from each regular supporter and can total £30 million a year.

The ninety-two clubs of the Premier and Football Leagues, the England squad and the FA generate £1 billion in merchandise sales.

In Rugby Union, merchandising centres largely on the sale of replica kits with a rather larger range of goods at the national headquarters of the game at Twickenham.

The RFU uses Twickenham to raise money, not only through gate money but also from corporate hospitality. The normal price for a good seat at an international match is £50 but the corporate price is currently £679. This buys the best seats and a three-course lunch for the clients.

Corporate hospitality generates 30 per cent of RFU revenue (more than television fees and ticket sales) and raised £25 million in 2006. The RFU markets 49,000 seats for every international match through its hospitality section, 'Twickenham Experience Ltd'. There are also around 6,000 hospitality packages on offer from rival companies so that every international generates £2.5 million for the RFU.

Independent companies buy 'unofficial' tickets from rugby clubs who receive an allocation from the RFU, the substantial profits going towards development of the sport at grass-roots level. Mike Burton, one of the leading hospitality providers, says that: 'We have built more clubhouses, car parks and pitches than I can remember by buying these tickets from the clubs. Match tickets are just about the only asset they have and they have to be able to cash them in'.

Corporate entertainment differs from corporate hospitality in that clients are involved in sporting activity, such as in 'pro-am' golf tournaments, which sees them playing alongside the stars and personalities of the game. Association with star players of other games can be arranged as part of a package designed to feed the ego of the client.

One of the most recent sports to employ this strategy is shooting and August each year sees the start of the sixteen-week pheasant-shooting season. Shooting with a musket was originally a very select sport, identifying the hunter as someone of substance and served as a 'badge of social superiority'. Companies who arrange this activity for clients today are in effect selling this badge and there are those who can afford their own 'badges' but still take part for the same reason. So, it is not unusual to find rock stars, American tourists and London financiers together on the moors.

Shooting parties were commonplace in Edwardian times as entertainment for house guests but today corporate entertainment agencies charge between £400 and £2,000 per person per day for the same privilege. Killing pheasants is one of the fastest growing sports with some 36 million birds reared each year in order to provide targets.

In 2006, there were more than 2,000 estates and farms offering shooting facilities. The business employs 25,000 people and has an estimated turnover of £600 million a year.

Keeping it clean

Clearly, sport today could not function without commercial sponsorship in one form or another. There are, however, too many examples of malpractice and deviance to ignore its corrupting influence.

In professional sport there is evidence of deviant attempts to enhance performance with well-publicised and high profile examples of drug-taking in cycling, swimming and athletics and of bribery in football, cricket and horse racing.

Since the last generates approximately £4.5 billion in betting revenue each year it is ripe with scandals about the doping of horses and the bribing of jockeys and stable staff. The gentlemanly side of racing is really something of a myth, arising initially from the participation of Charles II, who often rode on Newmarket Heath.

Horse racing is a multi-national business dominated by the Irish-based partnership of bloodstock expert John Magnier with the millionaire gambler Michael Tabor and Sheikh Mohammed Maktoum of Dubai. Their rivalry has fuelled a rise in world bloodstock prices and led to a greater commercialisation of horse breeding.

The dream is now not to win races for prize money and trophies but to enhance 'stud fees', which increase each time a horse wins. An established winner is paid £150,000 for every mare it 'covers' and thus great races have simply become a means to an end. As the Irish trainer Dermot Weld has said, 'racing used to be a fun game – now it's really just a business'.

In a sport that generates billions of pounds, the fees for riding (for most jockeys) are £50–61 for a ride on the flat and £80–84 'over the sticks'. A former Jockey Club head of security recently criticised the organisation as being 'institutionally corrupt' and lacking the 'moral courage and resolve' to deal with the sport's problems.

Even though its patron is the Queen, the Jockey Club has been investigated by the Gambling Review Board and the Office of Fair Trading and its influence over racing may be about to diminish considerably.

Whose sports are they?

Government agencies are having a much greater influence on the running of the sports industry than ever before. There was such concern in the 1990s that satellite television was buying up all the traditional sporting events, that a Government Advisory Board was established, which concluded that certain events, such as the FA Cup Final, the Derby and the Grand National, should be shown on BBC in order to 'maintain and foster a national community of interest'. The view of successive governments has been that sport:

■ boosts national identity and pride

■ strengthens communities

■ plays a key role in public health.

Government intervention

Today it seems that government intervention is welcomed. Participation at grass-roots level must be increased and national prestige demands international success.

The government feels that the free market will not necessarily bring about these twin objectives. The game of cricket seems to be failing, due largely to a fall in numbers playing the game in schools. A report in 1999 suggested that 'brownfield' sites should be used for development, which would mean even fewer areas where cricket could be played. For this and other reasons, the game is disappearing from inner-city schools along with some other sports. Inter-school fixtures have fallen by 70 per cent between 1995 and 2005.

The government response has been to inject £60 million into financing 600 Active School Co-ordinators to boost links between school sport and local sports clubs. Such interventions are necessary as sport becomes more commercialised and individualistic. People once kept fit by cycling, walking or kicking a ball around but now safe open spaces are in very short supply. Now, the fitness industry is creating 'privatised exercise', in that exercise clubs are open only to those who can pay the subscriptions.

The Physical Activity Task Force set up by government in 1999 under the auspices of the Department of Health reported that a quarter of school children are so unfit that they are likely to have heart conditions before they reach their thirties. If the Ministry of Defence needed to conscript recruits, as in 1900 and 1916, it might find the same levels of unfitness now as it did then.

The government also supports initiatives that might lead to the second objective of national prestige. The unsuccessful Manchester bid for the Olympic Games of 2000 cost around £8 million. Some of this came from commercial sponsors but

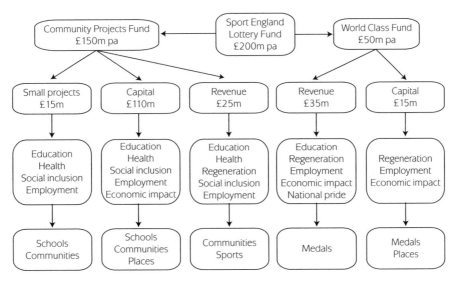

FIGURE 9.1   Sport England Lottery Fund: annual distribution

far more came from the government in grants. Since the National Lottery began the government has channelled some of this revenue directly into sport through the Sport England Lottery Fund.

The 1999–2009 strategy for this fund continues to place 'Sport for All' as an abiding principle but identifies two major themes for promotion:

■ to provide equality of opportunity for everyone, whatever their circumstances, to take part in sport

■ helping those with talent to develop into the sports stars of the future.

Grants from the sports lottery fund have now topped £1 billion and over 3,000 projects have been supported. This has resulted in, for example, a more than tripling of participation levels by the young and by women. Official Treasury figures claim that there has been a 28 per cent increase in sports funding since 2000.

The target for 2009 is to increase adult participation by 20 per cent with a similar increase in girls' participation levels. In élite sport the target is to improve on tenth place at the Athens Olympics and to gain a top four place at the London Olympics.

The next prestige project is the 2012 Olympics in London. Arup Consultants originally itemised the likely costs of such a venture as follows:

Expenditure:

   £779m to stage the event

   £403m to build the facilities

   £325m to buy the land

   £167m to improve UK medal chances

   £109m risk money to cover possible losses

Today, the costs have escalated to between £6 and £8 billion.

The decision to bid for the 2012 Olympic Games rested entirely with the government and was based almost entirely on non-sporting consideration. As Simon Clegg, CEO of the British Olympic Association says 'This is massive and goes way beyond sport. It has the potential to change the psyche of the nation in terms of how we look at ourselves. We're a winner here and the whole country's going to be a winner'.

If we look at the running total of sports industry turnover, we can see that of the £13.5 billion, all the factors to do with participation, such as equipment and subscriptions, account for £6.5 billion, whilst those related to spectators, such as admissions and television subscriptions, account for £7 billion.

It seems that very gradually we are beginning to take part in sport in greater numbers than before but critical sections of the community are being left behind. Ethnic minorities, women and girls are under-represented and, very worryingly,

TABLE 9.1   Sports industry 2006

Participation	Spectating
Largely public sector and voluntary	Largely private sector and commercial
Club membership	Television
Facilities (amateur, grass-roots)	Facilities (professional)
Equipment	Advertising and promotion
Shoes and clothing	Merchandising
Government policy (grass roots)	Government policy (prestige projects)
Club fund-raising	Betting
'Sportsmatch'	Commercial sponsorship
Governing bodies	Sports management companies
Total = £6.5 billion	Total = £7 billion

school-aged children are not taking up sports at all. Participation tends to come from men (and increasingly from women) of the relatively prosperous and growing middle class.

In the following and last chapter we shall try to explain the present situation by placing it in an appropriate historical context and sketch a scenario for our sporting future.

SPORT AS AN INDUSTRY

1   A 'professional attitude' to sport should refer to more than just winning. What might be meant by such a statement?

2   There has traditionally been a positive link between health and sport. Why is it that there are increasingly more 'fans' than participants?

3   If sport is now a business, why do we expect the successful businesses to give some of their (TV) money to the smaller less successful ones?

4   Historically, one argument in favour of televising sport was that it allowed more people to see it. Is this true of today's satellite broadcasts?

5   Is it realistic to expect sport to be conducted at a higher moral level than any other form of business?

6   Why do you think that present-day governments seem keener than their predecessors to be involved in sporting affairs?

Suggested further reading

Horrie, C., *Premiership – Lifting the Lid on a National Obsession* (Simon & Schuster, 2002)

Sport England, *Investing for Our Sporting Future: 1999–2009* (Sport England, 1999)

Vamplew, W., *Pay Up, Pay Up and Play the Game* (Cambridge University Press, 1988)

chapter ten

CONCLUSIONS

If one fact is evident from the foregoing review of English sport over eight centuries it is that no sport can be insulated from the wider society in which it is played.

We have seen that gentlemen have used their recreations as badges of social and physical superiority over the lower orders and we have also seen how this has been modified but maintained throughout the centuries.

If we accept the conclusion of William FitzStephen that all sport derives from a basic human inclination to play, then we must ask why the evolution of English sport has largely maintained the social and cultural differentials of so long ago.

A major shift of emphasis in the evolution of sport occurred when any activity indulged in for the 'sport' or fun of it was seen as socially disruptive and bad for the patriotic practice of archery. Thereafter, due to their unruly nature, all such indulgences were likely to be judged not only as 'un-English' but 'unmanly' and 'un-Christian'. Also of significance was that they were commonly played on Sundays.

The discipline imposed on society by a web of manorial rights and obligations extended to the recreational activities of ordinary people in an attempt to limit playful activities to those more consistent with genteel behaviour and civil obedience.

Gentlemanly recreations at that time were field sports, dancing and games of chance, all of which were founded in the ritual and regulation of courtly etiquette. Knowledge of such etiquette identified the player as socially superior to those who participated in similar activities from baser motives.

The hired man's field sports, founded on food gathering activities, were condemned as 'poaching', whilst his 'gambolling and betting' were dismissed as licentious and cited as evidence of inherent unreliability.

As activities like bowling and football became socially disruptive, the authorities sought to limit them by reducing free time and by outright prohibition. At the same time they made provision for regulated participation with the construction of football 'crofts' and bowling alleys.

Evidence of a genteel appropriation of popular sport is found in the introduction of football as a therapeutic exercise into some school curricula and in the laying of bowling greens. The decline of genteel interest in field archery resulted from the introduction of the musket, which joined the horse as a badge of superiority. The use of the musket for hunting was legitimised by the gentleman's 'game privilege', preserved by Charles II.

Regulating sport

Royalty had led the way in promoting horse racing but it became so popular that gentlemen sought to regulate it through the Jockey Club (1750). Its new regulations saw some taking up cricket as a less expensive form of gambling.

In appropriating cricket the gentry turned to a well-developed rural pursuit and continued the process with the enclosure of grounds following the establishment of the MCC in 1787. The MCC was a group of self-appointed metropolitan gentlemen who took it upon themselves to legislate for the game nationally.

The growth of mercantilism throughout the eighteenth century not only encouraged gentlemen to seek out gambling opportunities in their sports but also to commercialise them for profit. The promotion of race meetings also became a valued source of revenue for town councils up and down the country.

Genteel sponsorship of sport embraced cricket, horse racing, rowing, boxing and running, with the result that more sporting activities were enclosed, which facilitated payment and excluded undesirables. The first Thames Regatta (1775) took place out of public view between huge barges full of fee-paying aristocratic spectators. One result of this was the rise of the sporting journeyman who supplemented his trade income with prize-winnings and profits from gambling.

Betting involved 'fixing' and 'fouling', which became quite unacceptable to the first generation of 'muscular Christian' gentlemen educated in the newly revived public schools. The descent into pseudo-amateurism/pseudo-professionalism was accompanied by other developments that showed sport was evolving into business, with:

- cricket tours
- boxing bouts

- athletics meetings

- rowing regattas.

Sporting enclosures

This practice grew up as a result of the prodigious inflow of people into the newly urbanised areas – particularly London. This inflow, the result of the industrialisation of much of the country, provided both the demand for and the supply of sporting entertainment, which changed from open rural activities for participants to enclosed urban displays for paying spectators.

This change of style embodied the second major shift in the evolution of sport, that of competing for financial reward. The new generation of classically educated gentlemen condemned this activity on the basis that it encouraged 'unsporting' behaviour and was likely to set a bad example to society.

Gentlemen tried to halt the trend towards what they called 'the accursed greed for gold' (competing for money) in several ways, by:

- *licensing* sport in order to control it

- *prohibition* of certain activities by law

- *appropriating* games and 'gentrifying' them

- *withdrawing* themselves and their support from some activities.

As a result, the Victorian period saw huge growth in the number of sporting clubs with membership strictly limited to 'gentlemen amateurs'. Withdrawal into such clubs was the response of a middle class seeking to distance itself from the crowd. These clubs were unavailable to the working man for several reasons. They were:

- *socially* exclusive to members of certain professions or occupations

- *culturally* specific to 'genteel' behaviour

- *financially* far too expensive

- *geographically* often inaccessible.

The struggle for control of sport

In earlier centuries the landed gentry had maintained its distance with the help of feudal precedents and legal safeguards and in the seventeenth century the sporting club offered a haven of separate development.

Emulating the gentry of the seventeenth century, the *nouveau riche* of the nineteenth century strove to 'have some knowledge of all the arts but not to seek excellence in any'. They considered that anyone who practised enough to become excellent had ceased, in Trollope's words, 'to be a gentleman in the best sense'.

Thus, sportsmen who strove for excellence in order to win money became social outcasts and 'to keep them out was a thing desirable on every account'. For the gentlemen amateurs they represented as great a threat to the established order as the licentiousness of earlier times. Although the amateur ethic was successfully maintained in middle-class culture, this did not apply to football or rugby league, both of which were professionalised, and where working-class spectator demand justified payment to players.

The erosion of amateurism

The story of English sport in the twentieth century – particularly since 1945 – has been one of widespread erosion of amateurism. This has largely been due to the growth of international sport and to the development of television broadcasting. The first offered the prospect of enhanced prestige and the second provided huge financial incentives to both organisations and individuals.

The desire for international sporting success placed amateurs in a serious dilemma since it became obvious that they had no choice but to 'professionalise' in order to succeed. This process was expensive and explains why governing bodies increased their charges to affiliated clubs and made applications to the Sports Council for grants. The justification was 'the need to be more professional in order to remain amateur'.

The prospect of television fees and commercial sponsorship persuaded even the staunchly amateur bodies of athletics, rowing and rugby union to allow deferred payments to their players. This undermined their amateur credentials and associated them with that very 'greed for gold' that 'amateur' clubs had originally been established to eradicate.

The recent innovation of satellite television has brought the twin inducements of international prestige and financial gain to bear upon sport by offering staggering fees for participation in global competitions. Such inducements have lowered the amateur resolve of all those sports that have any spectator appeal. Even activities such as cricket, golf and tennis, which were appropriated as 'havens for gentlemen' in the nineteenth century, have succumbed to television offers and commercial sponsorship.

This movement towards a business culture based on the competitive success of élite sport groups in international 'leagues' of various kinds represents the third major shift in the evolution of domestic sport. At the same time, those activities once thought of as embodying the genteel purity of English leisure – the centuries-old field sports of hunting, shooting and fishing – have simply become part of our cultural heritage being sold off to Japanese, American and Arab businessmen.

Are the games the same?

In telling the story of English sport it is difficult to avoid the conclusion that, although the players may have changed, the tactics have remained remarkably similar. There is repeated evidence of this in situations that although shaped by modern circumstances are recognisable as the very essence of sport itself. The recreation of the human spirit through the joy of play has imbued all the activities visited in this survey. The ritualistic aspects of such behaviour can also be seen as clearly as ever:

- the licentiousness of early footballers destroying property has evolved into the hooliganism of football supporters destroying property in and around stadiums

- the efforts in the fifteenth century to stop such behaviour are mirrored almost exactly by those of recent times, exemplified in the Football Spectators Act of 1989

- the ritual of genteel recreations based on courtly etiquette gave rise to the formalisation of games organised by the gentlemen of the nineteenth century; they wished to emulate aristocracy in order to consolidate their own social position

- the inter-village tribalism of activities such as mediaeval Shrove Tuesday sports is still evident in the league competitions of various sports

- the cleavage between the north and south is still current, with, for example, southern favouritism being suspected in grant-aiding policies

- the high profile given to gambling as an investment in the eighteenth century is mirrored by the 'spread betting' of today's city analysts

- the therapeutic value of sport in schools, first recognised in the sixteenth century, now has a major role in government strategy for sport

- the mediaeval concept of authority presided over by God and represented on earth by the monarch, has its modern manifestation in government, Sport England, governing bodies, clubs and members

- sporting enclosures, which began in the fifteenth century, still raise money and control crowds; the Taylor Report of 1990 required £1 billion to be spent on their improvement

- public access to the countryside – brutally limited in mediaeval times – is still restricted today

- 'amateurism' is now practically obliterated by the financial inducements offered by global broadcasting

- the mediaeval popularity of football continues today – with 100,000 clubs in regular competition at grass-roots level

- a continued distrust of the foreign concept of sport, which often seems to omit the idea of 'fair play', is strengthened by corruption in the IOC

- women, who have been involved in sport since mediaeval times, continue to be under-represented and are given minimal press/TV coverage.

Sport for All

The above examples and many others serve to illustrate the dynamic nature of sport and the power it has to shape and reflect contemporary custom.

We have seen in preceding chapters that the evolution of English sport has had a recurring theme: that of exclusion. This has been inflicted on all identified as socially undesirable by the customs of succeeding generations.

These exclusions have been the result of petty snobbery, class selfishness, hypocrisy, religious bigotry, racism, sexism and xenophobia.

Since 1965 official government policy has been one of inclusion and 'Sport for All'.

Nevertheless, many continue to be excluded: including women, minority groups, school-aged children and the less well-off. It is regrettably true that the discrepancy between the 'Independent Class' and the 'Labouring Class', recorded in 1931, is almost exactly that which remains between 'Class 1' and 'Class 5' in the most recent survey of social trends.

The unchanging gap between the 'haves' and the 'have-nots' is graphically illustrated in the reference in Chapter Four, to a poor family of ten living on eighteen shillings (90p) a week, a sum that many gentlemen of the time would spend on one meal. One hundred and forty years later we might find similar allusions to the fact that many families on council estates eat for a week on the price of a single expense account lunch.

If this has been the story of the past and continues to be significant today, what can we say about the future of sport in England and, indeed, about society itself? The position of women in sport is still below that of men – mainly because the media virtually ignore them. Women's sport fails to attract significant levels of sponsorship as this is directly linked to television coverage, although this may be about to change since Paula Radcliffe became the BBC Sports Personality of the year in 2002 and Zara Phillips won the trophy in 2006.

It is also true to say that despite little media coverage, women's and girls' football is England's fastest growing sport with 800 women's teams affiliated to the FA and 1,800 girls' and 2,500 schoolgirls' teams also affiliated. The FA's 'Forward Plan' of 2002 promised to establish a women's professional league within a few years.

And what of the future...?

It is impossible to consider the future of any sport without contemplating the effect that television might have upon it.

A professional women's football league will only succeed with commercial sponsorship: which will only happen if games are televised. The FA must consider this before teams are established, players signed or fixtures organised.

Sports bodies have an uneasy relationship with broadcasters because they have conflicting objectives. The former look to protect their sport and generate funds for the long term, whilst the latter want to win ratings and sell satellite subscriptions. Television has had a range of effects upon sport:

- it has turned football into an international business but has forced many clubs into financial chaos

- it has brought about the death of boxing as a serious sport and culturally significant activity, producing what is regarded by many as simply a circus

- in promoting the big rugby league clubs it has marginalised many others and alienated many genuine fans

- it has turned cricket into a marketable product by emphasising its international aspects on pay-to-view channels. The County Championship, however, is in danger of being marginalised

- it has failed to revive dog racing as the mass spectator sport it used to be

- it has been responsible for making bowling into one of the most popular participant sports in the country

- it introduced skiing to the public and created a demand for skiing holidays abroad and dry ski slopes at home

- its coverage of tennis and golf continues to fuel the huge interest in these sports.

There are as many other examples as there are televised sports with supporters and detractors for each one. Some argue that television has brought much needed money into cricket whilst others feel that it has killed the 'spirit' of the game.

One result of the commercialisation of sport through television has been the depersonalisation of spectator sport with the old-fashioned 'fan' becoming simply a customer. The difference is that the fan cannot take his custom elsewhere whilst the customer can – and will!

This was poignantly expressed by a Leigh rugby league fan when his club was threatened with amalgamation with another local club: 'this would make a hole in my life that could never be filled'. In this particular case the feared amalgamation was avoided but, like many other rugby league clubs, Leigh had severe financial problems due to the cost of players and ground improvements, both the result of the higher standards demanded by television.

Once again, it is those who can afford to invest heavily that will benefit from television coverage whilst those who cannot will be bankrupted by it. Fortunately, the Leigh club found a saviour in a local business consortium that settled its debts of £500,000.

Inclusion and partnership

The future of the game of rugby league may be about to change radically. Sport England increased its pressure on the British Amateur Rugby League Association (BARLA) to accept proposals to re-unite with the Rugby Football League by threatening to withdraw its central funding of £130,000 per year. A policy of inclusion was strongly recommended to the two sides of the sport and (despite misgivings on the part of the amateurs, who felt that the professional clubs were acting solely in their own interest) a reunification was announced at the beginning of 2003.

An even greater degree of 'inclusion' may be necessary in the medium term as the financial necessities of bigger clubs might bring about the amalgamation of rugby union and rugby league after a separation of over 100 years. The future for many sports may of necessity involve such co-operation in an increasingly cut-throat industry.

A good example of co-operation is the new stadium in Hull, built 118 years after the first, funded through a share option scheme and promoted as a business proposition to entrepreneurs. The new stadium cost £27 million and was partly funded by the local council, which owns it and leases it to Hull City FC and Hull Rugby League Club who share its magnificent facilities.

An earlier and now well-established venture can be found at the other end of rugby league's 'M62 corridor' in the north Cheshire town of Widnes, where a new community stadium has replaced a facility that had been in continuous use since 1874. Again, the local council, with help from grant-aiding bodies, has helped create a facility that provides a playing venue for the Widnes rugby league club, Runcorn's non-league football club and Everton's reserves as well as a range of facilities for use by the local community.

It seems likely that other future developments will need to be funded by public/private initiatives and shared by different clubs, which will cut costs enormously. The treatment of clubs as merely commercial opportunities will also need to stop and a true partnership between supporters, communities, owners and sponsors will need to be forged.

According to Gordon Taylor of the PFA, clubs need to see their supporters as their first priority and not shareholders. The successful clubs are those centred in their own communities. This makes financial sense as it is fans passing through the turnstiles or those paying subscriptions and playing fees that provide the biggest single item of income for clubs in any sport.

Such co-operation will also be necessary at grass-roots level where clubs find it difficult to raise funds. Sponsorship is rarely forthcoming for such clubs and subscriptions never cover the running costs. Since the money available from Sport England via the lottery may not be from a bottomless pot it will be vital that clubs pool their resources and co-operate as much as possible. The administrators of the lottery fund have already said that in the future they will only provide substantial grant-aid for such ventures.

Addressing the need for change

One of the major problems encountered by those responsible for devising sports development strategies in England has been the complexity of the infrastructure. We play more sports in England than any other country – 140 of them – and for each sport there is a governing body, committees representing affiliated clubs, county and/or regional committees and an internal communication system which is seldom very efficient. There are disagreements on just how to make progress and often about just what progress really is anyway.

This bewildering diversity is the product of centuries of tradition, class division and a democratic temperament, all of which have bred a spirit of independence in both clubs and sporting institutions alike. Many sports hark back to a golden age of Corinthian amateurism and are still administered by passionate volunteers who have a distrust of outside interference. These people have often been called 'the blazer brigades' and targeted by critics as reactionaries holding back the tide of progress.

The outgoing director of Sport England did so in 2002 and concluded by commenting that 'many sports in England are run in an amateurish way and until they are modernised the country will never have any meaningful success'.

As an Australian he might reasonably offer this criticism but an inventory of sixty sports played internationally reveals that the UK is in fact ranked third in the world.

David Moffett was referring to world and Olympic championships in the major sports, in which we *are* sadly deficient for a country of around 60 million inhabitants.

Moffett himself represents one indication of modernisation – he comes from another country! One of English sport's traditional rejections was of 'foreign interference' and yet, recently, we have had quite a lot of it:

- Moffett at Sport England (Australia)
- Sven-Goran Eriksson – Football Association (Sweden)
- Jurgen Grobler – Amateur Rowing Association (Germany)
- Duncan Fletcher – English Cricket Board (Zimbabwe)
- Bill Sweetenham – Amateur Swimming Association (Australia)
- Patrice Hagelauer – Lawn Tennis Association (France)
- Four Football Premiership managers (France and Italy).

So it seems that at least part of the future of our sport will be the result of the inevitable growth of 'foreign influence'.

This influence is reflected in the Labour government's Strategy for Sport (December 2002) and followed the Prime Minister's resounding declaration at the Labour Party conference of 2000 that the government was preparing a sports policy which was also 'a health policy, an education policy, a crime policy and an anti-drugs policy'.

It seems that sport has finally been recognised as a universal force for good – it has to be said, not before time. The new strategy incorporates two foreign models for sport: the Finnish model, which advocates as many people as possible taking part in a wide variety of activities, and the Australian model, under which sports academies are set up with the aim of raising national pride by achieving international excellence.

Both of these models will have their origins in schools as £459 million is spent on an extensive development programme. There will be a network of specialist sports colleges (comprehensive schools with high-quality sports teaching), each of which will employ a school sports co-ordinator to liaise with up to ten other local schools. This will supplement other development work already linking school sport with after school activities at local clubs.

The government will also continue to provide grant aid to sports governing bodies so that they can establish centres of excellence in which future champions can be coached to stardom. It is to be hoped that the prospect of Olympic gold in 2012 will not detract from the pursuit of equally (arguably more) important efforts to improve participation at grass-roots level.

Undoing the damage

All of this is long overdue since school sport has been suffering since 1982 when the then government sanctioned the selling off of school playing fields to raise money for other school activities. Since then the deterioration in standards of physical education and school sport has been only too evident. There are some fairly grim facts concerning the present situation:

- the London borough of Camden, with a population of 300,000, has no green pitches available for use by children
- one in three primary schools no longer teaches swimming

- the British Heart Foundation says that a third of under-sevens fail to reach a recommended minimum level of physical activity

- by the age of fifteen, two-thirds of girls are so indolent as to be classified as inactive

- the proportion of children adjudged to be overweight has increased sevenfold in the last thirty years to 30 per cent

- seven out of ten school leavers abandon physical activity altogether.

The cost of Britain's physical inactivity has been calculated to be £2 billion per year when direct health costs are added to earnings lost due to sickness and premature mortality. Since 1982, involvement in certain areas of sporting activity has increased but those involved have been the relatively prosperous middle-aged who have the time to spend in recreational activities. The keep-fit business has exploded into prominence but other individual recreations have also increased, with participation rates (since 1985) reflecting this:

- hiking – 9 per cent of the population to 35 per cent

- swimming – 28 per cent to 60 per cent

- cycling – 15 per cent to 40 per cent

- fishing – 35 per cent to 65 per cent.

This growth in individual activities only reflects a similar movement in society at large. Team sports are declining, partly due to the situation in schools and partly to the increased cost of sport generally. It has been suggested that the growth in individual sports is a reaction to an increasingly depersonalised world. Witness the old-fashioned 'fan' becoming a thing of the past and the community of interest that he represented possibly disappearing with him.

This modern erosion of sporting allegiance only mirrors that of jobs, families and even nation states as we move inexorably towards a global village governed by international corporations where sport is owned and run by international management companies.

There is also a danger of sport dividing into two major factions: one is watched either live or on television by huge audiences as an entertainment and the other provides an outlet for the individual aspirations of those who have the time and money to exploit it.

Between these two groups lie almost 50 per cent of the population who continue to be excluded from regular participation. This group comprises (as we have seen) women, a variety of minority groups, school-aged children and the less well-off. The commercial sector is unlikely to seek their inclusion unless there is a profit to be made and even then perhaps as spectators rather than participants.

It seems likely that women will be targeted as having considerable commercial potential whilst others may have to rely on the voluntary and public sectors for any provision that might be made for them.

At the very beginning of the third millennium it is time that we learned the lesson of history, which carries a message for all of us. That message, which continues to be repeated loud and clear today, is that exclusion can breed resentment and disaffection with unfortunate results for the whole of society.

With that in mind, those in positions of influence must realise that the long-term future for both sport and society involves working together for the benefit of the whole community rather than divisively in the interests of a few. The nature of the 2002 strategy document on sport does seem to indicate that the government has understood this message. If so, we can conclude this narrative for the present in the hope that the story of sport in England will after all, have a happy ending.

QUESTIONS

CONCLUSIONS

1 'No sport can be insulated from the wider society in which it is played' – how do the changes in both sport and society in the last 100 years bear out this statement?

2 How have commercial influences changed the ways in which the public access sport?

3 Does the importance of international prestige and financial gain mean that sport has simply become too important to be left in the hands of sportsmen and women?

4 Sport needs space! How has this been provided in the past and how will it be provided in the future?

5 It is now often suggested that even top-level clubs should be prepared to share stadiums and/or other facilities. What are the advantages/ disadvantages of this?

6 Bearing in mind the part that exclusion has played in the history of English sport, is Sport for All a realistic aim?

APPENDIX: SYNOPSIS OF SPORTING EVOLUTION

Based on E. Yeo and S. Yeo: four means of repression of popular activities put forward in *Popular Culture* and *Class Conflict*:

- Joining and taking them over – appropriation;
- Organising rival activities – withdrawal;
- Licensing and pricing them – exclusion;
- Outright banning – prohibition.

Archery	Appropriated and priced largely out of reach in club structures.
Athletics	As pedestrianism it was often banned but as athletics it was later appropriated as an Olympic sport.
Bowling	Banned as socially disruptive but appropriated by the leisured class and largely abandoned when popularly available.
Boxing	As pugilism it was often banned but as boxing it was appropriated as the 'noble art'; later abandoned owing to fixing.
Cricket	Appropriated and priced largely out of reach in club culture.
Cycling	Initially appropriated, subsequently licensed but soon abandoned owing to popularity; withdrawal to motor sports.
Fishing	Banned and/or licensed; growth of popularity forced withdrawal from coarse fishing into game fishing, which was priced out of reach.
Football	Banned and appropriated, subsequently abandoned at the onset of professionalism in favour of rugby union.

Golf	Appropriated and priced out of reach in club culture.
Hockey	Appropriated and developed in a club culture.
Hunting	Banned and/or licensed and priced out of reach.
Racing	The 'sport of kings', always of privileged access, continues to be run in the interests of the owners.
Rowing	Appropriated and gentrified and priced out of reach in clubs.
Rugby	Established as an amateur alternative to football into which gentlemen withdrew; priced out of reach in club culture.
Shooting	Banned and/or licensed and priced out of reach.
Swimming	Initially appropriated as therapeutic but abandoned following mass popularity and availability.
Tennis	Appropriated and priced out of popular reach in club culture.

Note: The above helps to explain why those sports that either have maintained open access or were not susceptible to regulation are now the most popular participation sports, i.e. athletics (all forms of running), bowling, cycling, fishing and swimming.

BIBLIOGRAPHY

Individual sports

Altham, R. and Swanton, J., *A History of Cricket* (Allen & Unwin, 1962)

Anon., *Treatyse on Fyssinge* (Anon., 1496)

Ascham, R., *Toxophilus* (1545) (Scolar Press [facsimile] 1971)

Batchelor, D., *British Boxing* (Faber, 1940)

Bellamy, R., *The Story of Squash* (Cassell, 1976)

Bird, D., *Our Skating Heritage* (National Skating Association, 1979)

Brailsford, D., *A Social History of Prize Fighting* (Lutterworth, 1988)

Brookes, C., *English Cricket* (Weidenfeld & Nicolson, 1978)

Browning, R., *A History of Golf* (Allen Lane, 1956)

Burke, E., *The History of Archery* (Fawcett Muller, 1958)

Cardus, N. and Arlott, J., *The Noblest Game* (Longman, 1969)

De Beaumont, R., *Fencing, Ancient Art and Modern Sport* (Kaye Ward, 1970)

Denison's Cricketers' Companion, 1845

Digby, E., *Scientific Treatise on Swimming* (London, 1587)

Downer, A.R., *Running Recollections* (Blairgowrie Books, 1982)

Fleischer, N., *A History of Heavyweight Boxing, 1719 to the Present* (Putnam, 1949)

Gate, R., *Rugby League* (Arthur Barker, 1989)

Grimsley, W., *Tennis, its History, People and Events* (Prentice, 1971)

Harding, J., *For the Good of the Game* (Robson Books, 1991)

Harris, H.A., *Greek Athletes and Athletics* (Hutchinson, 1964)

Hawkes, J., *The Meynellian Science* (Leicester University Press, 1932)

Heath, E.G., *A History of Target Archery* (David & Charles, 1973)

Hill, C., *Horse Power, the Politics of the Turf* (Manchester University Press, 1988)

Horrie, C., *Premiership – Lifting the Lid on a National Obsession* (Simon & Schuster, 2002)

Itzkovitz, D., *Peculiar Privilege: A Social History of English Fox-Hunting* (Hassocks, 1977)

Lake, A. and Wright, D., *Bibliography of Archery* (Manchester University Press, 1988)

Lemon, D., *The Crisis of Captaincy* (Christopher Helm, 1988)

Longrigg, R., *A History of Horse Racing* (Macmillan, 1972)

Lord Aberdare, *The Book of Tennis and Raquets* (Stanley Paul, 1980)

Lunn, A., *The Story of Skiing* (Eyre & Spottiswoode, 1952)

Lunn, A., *A Century of Mountaineering* (Allen & Unwin, 1957)

Lyttleton, B. and Padwick, E., *A Bibliography of Cricket* (Clarke, 1977)

Macklin, K., *The History of Rugby League* (Stanley Paul, 1974)

Malherbe, W., *A Chronological Bibliography of Hockey* (Hockey Association, 1965)

Marshall, M., *Gentlemen and Players* (Grafton, 1987)

Mason, A., *Association Football and English Society 1863–1915* (Harvester, 1980)

McNab, T., *A History of Professional Athletics* (Athletics Association, 1972)

Moorbouse, G., *Lords* (Hodder & Stoughton, 1983)

Mortimer, R., *The Jockey Club* (Cassell, 1958)

Mortimer, R., *A History of the Derby Stakes* (Joseph, 1962)

Owen, O.L., *The History of the Rugby Football Union* (Playfair, 1955)

Philips-Birt, D., *The Cumberland Fleet* (David & Charles, 1975)

Robertson, M., *Wimbledon, 1877–1977* (Arthur Barker, 1977)

Rowley, P., *The Book of Hockey* (Batsford, 1963)

Scott, J., *The Athletic Revolution* (Free Press, 1971)

Seth-Smith, M., *A History of Steeple-Chasing* (Joseph, 1966)

Shearman, M., *Athletics* (Longman Green, 1889)

Sissons, R., *The Player: A Social History of the Professional Cricketer* (Kingswood Press, 1988)

Smith, R., *A Social History of the Bicycle* (American Heritage, 1972)

Smyth, J., *Lawn Tennis* (Batsford, 1966)

Solomon, J.W., *Croquet* (Batsford, 1966)

Surtees, R.S., *Analysis of the Hunting Field* (White, 1830)

Tabner, B., *Through the Turnstiles* (Yore Publications, 1993)

Thomas, P., *The Northern Cross Country Association, Centenary History* (NCCA, 1982)

Thompson, L., *The Dogs: A Personal History of Greyhound Racing* (Chatto & Windus, 1994)

Vamplew, W., *Pay Up, Pay Up and Play the Game* (Cambridge University Press, 1988)

Walvin, J., *The People's Game: A Social History of British Football* (Arrow Books, 1975)

Watman, M., *A History of British Athletics* (Hale, 1968)

Whyte, J.C., *A History of the British Turf* (Longman, 1840)

Wigglesworth, N., *A Social History of English Rowing* (Cass, 1992)

Collected works on sport

Arlott, J., *The Oxford Companion to Sports and Games* (Paladin, 1977)

Bale, J., *Sport and Place: A Geography of Sport* (Hurst & Co., 1982)

Briggs, A., *Essays in the History of Publishing* (Longman, 1974)

Burke, P., *Popular Culture in Early Modern Europe* (Temple Smith, 1978)

Burrows, H. and Wood, L., *Sports and Pastimes in English Literature* (Nelson, 1925)

Cone, C. (ed.), *Sundry Sports of Merry England* (Kentucky University Press, 1981)

Cox, R., *Sport: A Guide to Historical Sources in the UK* (Sports Council Information Series No. 9, 1983)

Ford, J., *This Sporting Land* (New English Library, 1977)

Fulford, R. (ed.), *The Greville Memoirs* (Batsford, 1963)

Goodman, P., *Sporting Life: An Anthology of British Sporting Prints* (British Museum, 1983)

Harris, H.A., *Sport in Britain* (Stanley Paul, 1975)

Lady Greville, *The Gentlewomen's Book of Sports* (Spalding, 1880)

King James I, *Book of Sports* (London, 1617)

Lennox, W., *Pictures of Sporting Life and Character* (Hurst, 1860)

Longrigg, R., *The English Squire and his Sport* (Joseph, 1977)

McCrone, K., 'Sport at the Oxbridge Women's Colleges to 1914' (*British Journal of Sports History*, September 1986)

MacLaren, A., *Training in Theory and Practice* (Macmillan, 1866)

Nickalls, G.O., *With the Skin of Their Teeth* (Country Life, 1951)

Peek, H., *The Poetry of Sport* (Longman & Co., 1896)

Reekie, H.M., 'A History of Sport and Recreation for Women in Great Britain, 1770–1850' (Ohio State University, PhD, 1982)

Rodgers, H.B., *Pilot National Recreation Survey* (Keele University, 1966)

Trollope, A., *British Sports and Pastimes* (Virtue, 1868)

Vale, M., *The Gentlemen's Recreations 1580–1630* (Brewer, 1977)

Walsh, J.H., *A Manual of British Rural Sports* (Routledge, 1856)

Whitney, C., *A Sporting Pilgrimage to Oxford, Cambridge and the Shires* (Osgood McIlvaine, 1894)

Social commentary

Allison, L., *The Politics of Sport* (Manchester University Press, 1986)

Arnold, J., 'The Influence of Pilkington Brothers on Sport and Community in St Helens' (MEd, Liverpool University, 1977)

Aspin, D., 'The Nature and Purpose of Sporting Activity' (*Physical Education Review*, Spring 1986)

Bailey, P., *Leisure and Class in Victorian England* (Routledge, 1978)

Ball, D. and Loy, J., *Sport and Social Order* (Addison Wesley, 1975)

Benson, G., *Towards Social Reform* (Longman Green, 1909)

Berryman, J.W., 'Sport as Social History' (*Quest*, Summer 1973)

Bert, E., *An Approved Treatise on Hawking* (London, 1619)

Blanchard, E. and Cheska, P., *The Anthropology of Sport* (Bergin Garvey, 1985)

Brailsford, D., *Some Factors in the Evolution of Sport* (Lutterworth, 1993)

Brooke-Smith, M., 'The Growth and Development of Popular Entertainment in the Lancashire Cotton Towns 1830–1870' (MLitt, Lancaster University, 1971)

Cardus, N., *Cardus on Cricket* (Souvenir Press, 1977)

Carter, J., *Sports and Pastimes of the Middle Ages* (University Press of America, 1988)

Cashman, E. and McKernan, R., *Sport in History* (Queensland University Press, 1979)

Chataway, C. and Goodhart, G., *War Without Weapons* (Allen, 1968)

Clarke, J., *The Devil Makes Work: Leisure in Capitalist Britain* (Illinois University Press, 1985)

Cross, G., *A Social History of Leisure Since 1600* (Venture, 1990)

Cunningham, H., *Leisure in the Industrial Revolution* (Croom, 1980)

Dando, J. and Runt, H., *Banks Bay Horse in Trance* (London, 1595)

Defoe, D., 'A tour through the whole island of Great Britain' (London, 1726)

Dobbs, B., *Edwardians at Play* (Pelham, 1973)

Donajgrodski, J., *Social Control in Nineteenth-Century England* (Croom, 1980)

Dunning, E. and Sheard, K., *Barbarians, Gentlemen and Players* (Robertson, 1979)

Dunning, E., Maguire, J. and Pearson, G., *The Sports Process: A Comparative and Developmental Approach* (Routledge, 1993)

Ensor, E., 'The Football Madness' (*Contemporary Review*, lxxiv, 1898)

Fane, A. Lady, *Chit Chat* (Methuen, 1926)

Fitzstephen, W., *History of London* (London, c. 1175)

Ford, J., *This Sporting Land* (New English Library, 1977)

Golby, J. and Purdue, A., *The Civilisation of the Crowd: Popular Culture in England, 1750–1900* (Batsford, 1984)

Haley B., 'Sports and the Victorian World' *(Western Humanities Review,* 22, 1968)

Haley, B., *The Healthy Body and Victorian Culture* (Harvard University Press, 1978)

Hammond, L. and Hammond, B., *The Age of the Chartists 1832–1854* (Anchor, 1962)

Hargreaves, J., *Sport, Power and Culture* (Polity Press, 1986)

Hawkins, B. and Lowerson, J., *Trends in Leisure* (Sussex University Press, 1979)

Holt, R., *Sport and the British* (Oxford University Press, 1989)

Holt, R., *Sport and the Working Class in Modern Britain* (Manchester University Press, 1992)

Ingham, R. and Loy, J., *Sport in Social Development* (Hutchinson, 1993)

James, C.L.R., *Beyond a Boundary* (Hutchinson, 1963)

Krawczyk, B., 'Social Origin and Ambivalent Character of Ideology of Amateur Sport' (*International Review of Sport Sociology,* vol. 2,1977)

Lang, C.G., *Sermons* (Nelson 1913)

Lowerson, J., *Sport and the English Middle Classes* (Manchester University Press, 1993)

Lowerson, J. and Myerscough, G., *Time to Spare in Victorian England* (Harvester Press, 1977)

Lucas, J., *The Future of the Olympic Games* (Routledge, 1992)

Malcolmson, R., *Popular Recreations in English Society 1700–1850* (Cambridge University Press, 1973)

Mangan, J., *Athleticism in the Victorian and Edwardian Public School* (Cambridge University Press, 1981)

Mangan, J., *The Cultural Bond: Sport, Empire and Society* (Frank Cass, 1992)

Mangan, J. and Park, B., *Pleasure, Profit and Proselytism* (Frank Cass, 1988)

Mangan, J. and Park, B., *From Fair Sex to Feminism* (Frank Cass, 1992)

Marx, K., *Capital* (Lawrence & Wishart, 1970)

Mason, A., *Sport in Britain* (Faber & Faber, 1988)

McCrone, K., *Sport and the Physical Emancipation of English Women* (Lutterworth Press, 1988)

McIntosh, P., *Sport in Society* (Watts, 1963)

McIntosh, P., 'Historical View of Sport and Social Control' (*International Review of Sport Sociology,* Vol. 6, 1973)

McIntosh, P., *Fair Play: Ethics in Sport and Education* (Heinemann, 1979)

Mellor, H., *Leisure and the Changing City 1870–1914* (Routledge, 1976)

Metcalfe, A., 'Sport in Nineteenth-Century England' (PhD, Wisconsin University, 1968)

Midwinter, E., *Fair Game* (Allen and Unwin, 1986)

Mulcaster, R., *The Schoolmaster* (London, 1561)

Natan, A., *Sport and Society* (Bowes and Bowes, 1958)

Pimlott, J., *Recreations* (Studio Vista, 1968)

Pimlott, J., *An Englishman's Holiday* (Harvester Press, 1976)

Plumb, J., *The Growth of Leisure 1630–1830* (Oxford University Press, 1972)

Plumb, J., *The Commercialisation of Leisure in the Eighteenth Century* (Reading University Press, 1974)

Rees, R., 'The Development of Physical Recreation in Liverpool in the Nineteenth Century' (MA Thesis, Liverpool University, 1968)

Roberts, J., *The Commercial Sector in Leisure* (Sports Council, 1979)

Roberts, J., *The Economic Impact of Sport in the UK* (Henley Centre for Economic Forecasting, 1992)

Simson, A., *The Lords of the Rings* (Simon and Schuster, 1992)

Smith, S., 'Remarks on the System of Education in Public Schools' (*Edinburgh Review*, Vol. XVI, August 1810)

Strutt, J., *The Sports and Pastimes of the People of England* (White, 1801)

Talbot, M., *Women and Leisure* (Sports Council, 1979)

Tomlinson, A. and Tomlinson, M., *Insights into Leisure and Culture* (Sports Council, 1984)

Trollope, A., *British Sports and Pastimes* (Virtue, 1868)

Trollope, A., *The New Zealander* (Clarendon Press, 1972)

Walton, J., *The English Seaside Resort, 1750–1914* (Leicester University Press, 1983)

Walton, J. and Walvin J., *Leisure in Britain* (Manchester University Press, 1983)

Walvin, J., *Beside the Sea* (Allen Lane, 1978)

Walvin, J., *Leisure and Society* (Longman, 1978)

Walvin, J., *Football and the Decline of Britain* (Macmillan, 1986)

Waszack, P., 'The Development of Leisure and Cultural Facilities in Peterborough, 1850–1900' (BA, Huddersfield Polytechnic, 1972)

Whitney, C., *A Sporting Pilgrimage to Oxford, Cambridge and the Shires* (Osgood McIlvaine, 1894)

Wood, A., *Memoirs of the Holles Family* (Camden, 3rd series, 1937)

Wood, H. and Burrows, H., *Sports and Pastimes in English Literature* (Nelson, 1925)

Worsley, T., *Barbarians and Philistines* (Robert Hale, 1940)

Worsley, T., *The End of the Old School Tie* (Secker & Warburg, 1941)

Yeo, E. and Yeo, S., *Popular Culture and Class Conflict* (Harvester, 1981)

Cultural background

Adams, R., *Paradoxical Harvest: Energy and Explanation in British History 1870–1914* (Cambridge University Press, 1982)

Baumann, Z., *Memories of Class* (Routledge and Kegan Paul, 1982)

Beeton, Mrs, *The Book of Household Management* (1888) (rep. Cape, 1968)

Lady Bell, *At the Works – A Study of a Manufacturing Town* (Arnold, 1907)

Benson, J., *The Working Class in England 1875–1914* (Croom Helm, 1985)

Briggs, A., *Victorian Cities* (Odhams, 1963)

Campbell, R., *The London Tradesman* (1747) (rep. Kelly, 1969)

Cannadine, D., *Patricians, Power and Politics in Nineteenth-Century Towns* (Leicester University Press, 1982)

Cannon, J., *Aristocratic Century, The Peerage of 18th-Century England* (Cambridge University Press, 1984)

Chandos, J., *Boys Together, English Public Schools 1800–1864* (Hutchinson, 1984)

Checkland, S., 'English Provincial Cities' (*Economic History Review*, January 1954)

Christie, I., *Stress and Stability in Late Eighteenth-Century Britain* (Oxford University Press, 1985)

Cole, J. and Postgate, R., *The Common People* (Methuen, 1961)

Crouch, C., *The Scope for Socialism* (Fabian Society, 1985)

Daverson, J. and Lindsay, K., *Voices from the Middle Class* (Hutchinson, 1975)

Davidoff, L., *The Best Circles* (Croom Helm, 1973)

Davidoff, L. and Hall, C., *Family Fortunes: Men and Women of the English Middle Class, 1780–1850* (Hutchinson, 1985)

Davis, I., *The Harlot and the Statesman* (Kensal Press, 1987)

Dore, L. and Jerrold, M., *In London – A Pilgrimage* (Grant, 1872)

d'Ormesson, J., *Grand Hotel* (Dent, 1984)

Dunkereley, D., *Occupations and Society* (Routledge and Kegan Paul, 1975)

Dyson, A. and Lovelock, J., *Education and Democracy* (Routledge and Kegan Paul, 1975)

Escott, T., *Social Transformations of the Victorian Age* (Seeley & Co., 1897)

Evans, E., *Social Policy 1830–1914* (Routledge and Kegan Paul, 1978)

Fried, G. and Elman, P., *Charles Booth's London* (Hutchinson, 1969)

Fulford, R., *The Greville Memoirs* (Batsford, 1963)

Gash, N., *Aristocracy and People* (Arnold, 1985)

Gay, J., *Trivia et al.* (rep. Fyfield Books, 1979)

Grego, J., *Rowlandson, the Caricaturist* (Chatto, 1880)

Hampden, J., *An Eighteenth-Century Journal 1774–1776* (Macmillan, 1940)

Harrison, B., *Drink and the Victorians* (Faber, 1971)

Harrison, B., *Peaceable Kingdom* (Clarendon Press, 1982)

Hawker, J., *The Journal of a Victorian Preacher* (Oxford University Press, 1961)

Hayes, J., *Rowlandson: Watercolours and Drawings* (Phaidon, 1972)

Heald, T., *Networks* (Hodder & Stoughton, 1983)

Hecht, J., *The Domestic Servant Class in Eighteenth-Century England* (Routledge and Kegan Paul, 1956)

Henisch, B., *Cakes and Characters* (Prospect Books, 1984)

Heward, C., *Making a Man of Him: Parents and Their Sons' Education at an English Public School 1929–1950* (Routledge, 1988)

Hibbert, C., *The English – A Social History* (Grafton, 1986)

Himmlefarb, G., *The Idea of Poverty* (Faber, 1984)

Hopkins, H., *The Long Affray* (Secker & Warburg, 1979)

Jeffries, S., *The Spinster and her Enemies 1880–1930* (Pandora, 1985)

Jenkins, P., *The Making of a Ruling Class 1640–1790* (Cambridge University Press, 1983)

Lansdell, A., 'Costume for Oarswomen 1919–1979' (*Costume*, No. 13, 1979)

Lauwerys, J., 'The Philosophical Approach to Comparative Education' (*International Review of Education*, Vol. 5, 1959)

Lorimer, D., *Colour, Class and the Victorians* (Leicester University Press, 1978)

Mann, M., *Socialism Can Survive* (Fabian Society, 1985)

Mantoux, P., *The Industrial Revolution in the Eighteenth Century* (Methuen, 1964)

Marsh, D., *The Changing Structure of England and Wales* (Routledge, 1965)

Mingay, C., *The Transformation of Britain* (Routledge and Kegan Paul, 1986)

Munsche, P., *Gentlemen and Poachers 1671–1831* (Cambridge University Press, 1981)

Neale, R., *Class and Ideology in the Nineteenth Century* (Routledge, 1972)

Newby, H., *Country Life: A Social History of Rural England* (Weidenfeld, 1987)

Owen, C., *Social Stratification* (Routledge and Kegan Paul, 1968)

Paulson, R., *Hogarth, His Life and Times* (Yale University Press, 1971)

Payne, P., *British Entrepreneurship in the 19th Century* (Routledge, 1974)

Pearson, G., *Hooligan: A History of Respectable Fears* (Macmillan, 1983)

Penn, R., *Skilled Workers in the Class Struggle* (Cambridge University Press, 1984)

Pepys, S., *Diary* (Bell & Hyman, 1973)

Perkin, H., 'The Origins of the Popular Press' (*History Today*, Vol. 7, 1957)

Perkin, H., *The Origins of Modern English Society 1780–1880* (Routledge, 1969)

Perkin, H., *The Social Tone of Victorian Seaside Resorts in North West England* (University of Lancaster Press, 1976)

Perkin, H., *Professionalism, Property and English Society since 1880* (Reading University Press, 1981)

Perkin, H., *The Structured Crowd* (Harvester Press, 1981)

Philips, K., *Language and Class in Victorian England* (Blackwell, 1984)

Pick, J., *The West End: Mismanagement and Snobbery* (Offord, 1984)

Plumb, J., *The Birth of a Consumer Society: The Commercialisation of 18th-Century England* (Hutchinson, 1983

Read, D., *The English Provinces 1760–1960* (Arnold, 1964)

Reed, M., *The Georgian Triumph 1700–1830* (Routledge and Kegan Paul, 1983)

Richards, J. and Mackenzie, J., *A Social History of the Railway Station* (Oxford University Press, 1986)

Roberts, E., *A Woman's Place 1890–1940* (Blackwell, 1984)

Robinson, J., *The Latest Country Houses 1945–1983* (Bodley Head, 1985)

Robson, B., *Where is the North?* (City of Manchester, 1985)

Sanderson, M., *The Universities in the 19th Century* (Routledge and Kegan Paul, 1975)

Scott, A., *The Early Hanoverian Age 1714–1760* (Croom Helm, 1980)

Sharpe, J., *Crime in Early Modern England 1550–1750* (Longman, 1984)

Stanley, L., *The Diaries of Hannah Cullwick* (Virago, 1984)

Stevenson, J., *English Urban History 1500–1780* (Open University Press, 1982)

Stone, L. and Stone, J., *An Open Elite* (Oxford University Press, 1986)

Walker, S., *Sporting Art 1740–1900* (Studio Vista, 1972)

Wigley, J., *The Rise and Fall of the Victorian Sunday* (Manchester University Press, 1980)

Wingfield, R., *Victorian Sunset* (Murray, 1932)

Wright, T., *Some Habits and Customs of the Working Class* (rep. Kelly, 1967)

Club/society minutes

Alcester Cricket Club, Warwick County Records Office, Warwick, CV34 4JS (Ref. CRI *14An43*)

Alnmouth Golf Club, Northumberland Record Office, Newcastle, NE3 5QX (Ref. NRO 30.201438)

Anson Hunt Races, William Salt Library, Stafford, ST16 2LZ

Appleby Golf Club, Cumbria Record Officer, Kendal, LA9 4RQ (Ref. WDSO/40)

Astley Bowling Club, Tameside Local Studies Dept., Stalybridge, SK15 2BN (Ref. DD 37)

Bebington Bowling Club, Birkenhead Reference Library, L41 2XB (Ref. YBB)

Beccles Golf Club, Suffolk Records Officer, Ipswich, IP4 2JS (Ref. HD49 4051122)

Bedale Bowling Club, North Yorkshire County Record Office, Northallerton, DL7 8AD

Bellingham Bowling and Lawn Tennis Club, Lewisham Archives, Lewisham, SE13 5SY

Blackheath Hockey Club, Lewisham Archives, Lewisham, SE13 5SY

Bolton Cricket Club, Bolton Metropolitan Borough Archives, BL1 1SA (Ref. 22/193)

Bolton Municipal Officers Rifle Club, Bolton Metropolitan Archives, BL1 1SA (Ref. FZ/I)

Bolton Playing Fields Society, Bolton Metropolitan Borough Archives, BL1 1SA (Ref. S3/17)

Bolton Rugby Football Club, Bolton Metropolitan Borough Archives, BL1 1SA (Ref. 22/243)

Bolton Swimming Club, Bolton Metropolitan Borough Archives, BL1 1SA (Ref. FZ/8)

Bowmen of Edgbaston, Birmingham Reference Library, B3 3HQ

Bristol Cyclists Touring Club, Bristol Record Office, BS1 5TR (Ref. 31415(7))

Bristol Long Range Club, Bristol Record Officer, BS1 5TR

Bullingdon Club, Wiltshire Record Office, Trowbridge, BA14 8OG (Ref. WRO 947)

Bungay Steeple Chase, Suffolk Records Office, Ipswich, IP4 2JS (Ref. HD49 405/118)

Casterton Rifle Club, Cumbria Record Office (WDSO/87)

Catford Cycling Club, Lewisham Archives, Lewisham, SE13 5SY

Caxton Cricket Club, Cambridge Record Office, CB2 OAP (P37/2411)

Cestreham Cycling Club, Buckinghamshire Record Office, Aylesbury, HP20 1HA (D/ x 566)

Cheltenham Cycling Club, Gloucestershire Record Office, Gloucester, GL1 3DW

Corinthian Sailing Club, Hammersmith Archives, London, W12 8LJ

Crosthwaite Bowling Club, Cumbria Record Office, Kendal, LA9 4RQ (WDS0n)

Cumberland and Westmorland Wrestling Society, Cumbria Record Office (D/ S0/48)

Darlington Archers, Darlington Public Library, DL1 1ND (DIX/D30)

Darlington Billiard Club, Darlington Public Library, DL1 1ND (D/X/22)

Darlington Cycling Club, Darlington Public Library, DL1 1ND (D/HP/109-1 10)

Didsbury Archers, Manchester City Archives, M2 5PD (M6211/2)

Didsbury Archers and Hunters, Manchester City Archives, M2 5PD (M621112)

Didsbury Bowling Green, Manchester City Archives, M2 5PD (M621112)

Dresden Boat Club, Nottinghamshire Record Office, NGI IHR (DDBB 119)

Dunmow Tennis Club, Essex Record Office, CM5 1LX (DIDW 23)

Dunmow Park Tennis Club, Essex Record Office, CM5 1LX (D/DW 23)

Durham City Cricket Club, Durham County Records, DH1 5UL (DIDCC)

Durham Cyclists Touring Club, Durham County Records, DH1 5UL (D/DCT)

Durham National Playing Fields Association, Durham County Records, DH1 5UL
(D/IAH 101131 1/1–6)

Fambridge Yacht Club, Essex Record Office, BM1 1LX (D/226)

Finsbury Park Cycling Club, Haringey Museum, N17 8NU

Fleetwood Gala, Lancaster City Archives, LA1 4AW

Fulwood Race Course, Lancashire Records Office, Preston, PR1 5ND
(DDX/03/4)

Gateshead Fox Hounds, Northumberland Records, NE3 5QX (ZSI.316)

Gloucestershire County Cricket Club, Minutes for 1879, Gloucestershire Records
Office, GL1 3SY (GCC M/79)

Hambledon Cricket Club, Hampshire Record Office, SO23 9EF (F/239)

Headingley Bowling Club, Leeds Archives, LS7 3AP (1978)

Henley Royal Regatta, Regatta Headquarters, Henley-on-Thames

Hexham Steeplechase, Northumberland Records, NE3 5QX (ZMD 2115)

Hinton St George Cricket Club, Somerset Records, TA2 7PU (DD/HWIZ)

Holme Athletic Sports, Cumbria Records Office, Kendal, LA9 4RQ (WDSO/37)

Hull Athletic Ground Company, Kingston on Hull Record Office, HU1 1HN
(DBHT/91390)

Hutton in the Forest Cricket Club, Cumbria Records, Carlisle, CA3 8UR (Vane
Family Collection)

Huyton Cricket Club, Knowsley Central Library, Liverpool, L36 9DJ

Irthing Vale Wanderers Cricket Club, Cumbria Records, Carlisle, CA3 8UR (D/
S0/9)

John O'Gaunt Bowmen, Lancashire Records Office, Preston, PR1 2RE

John O'Gaunt Rowing Club, Lancashire Records Office, Preston, PR1 2RE

Jolly Anglers Society, Central Library, Warrington, WA1 1JB

Kempsford Cricket Club, Gloucestershire Records, GL1 3DW

Kendal Amateur Swimming Club, Cumbria Records Office, Kendal, LA9 4RQ
(WDSO/10)

Kendal Ladies Hockey Club, Cumbria Records Office, Kendal, LA9 4RQ
(WDSO/10)

Kendal Rugby Union Football Club, Cumbria Records Office, Kendal, LA9 4RQ
(WDSO/80)

Kendal Skating Club, Cumbria Records Office, Kendal, LA9 4RQ (WD/RG)

Kindon Football Club, Dorset Records Office, DT1 1XJ (P362/PCCI)

Lake Hatherton Fishery, William Salt Library, Stafford, ST16 2LZ

Lambton Tally Ho Club, Durham County Records, DH1 5UL (D/lo/F 1013)

Lancaster Football Club, Lancashire Records, Preston, PR1 2RE (DDX 411135)

Lancaster Golf Club, Lancashire Records Office, Preston, PR1 2RE (DDX 411136)

Lancaster Races, Lancashire Records Office, Preston, PR1 2RE (DDX 441132)

Lancaster Regatta, Lancashire Records Office, Preston, PR1 2RE

Lichfield Races, William Salt Library, Stafford, ST16 2LZ

Linton Sports, Cambridgeshire Records, CB2 0AP (L95/15A)

Maldon Bicycle Club, Essex Records, Chelmsford, CM5 1LX (T/A475)

Mersey Archery Society, Manchester City Archives, M2 5PD (M564511-3)

Minnesingens Yacht Club, Portsmouth City Records, P01 2LE

Morpeth Olympic Games,, Northumberland Records, NE3 5QX (NRO 1565)

Moseley United Bowling Club, Birmingham Reference Library, B3 3HO

National Fitness Campaign, Tyne and Wear Archives, NE1 4JA (1407)

Netherfield Amateur Swimming Club, Cumbria Records, LA9 4RQ (WDSO/71)

Newton Heath Racecourse, Records held at the Racecourse, Haydock

North Staffordshire Hunt, Staffordshire Record Office, ST16 2LZ (Colonel Dobson Collection)

Northumberland Cockfighting, Northumberland Records, NE3 5QX (ZALA 19)

Oken Bicycle Club, Warwick County Records, CV34 4JS (CRI 844)

Old Raby Hunt, Durham County Records, DH1 5UL (D/St/V 1633)

Park Swimming Club, Haringey Museum, N17 8NU

Porlock Golf Club, Somerset Records, Taunton, TA2 7PU (DDBR/6n33)

Preston Mutual Improvement Society, Lancashire Records, PR1 8ND (DDX 411137)

Professional Footballer's Union, PFU Headquarters, Manchester, M2 3WQ

Quayside Sports (Lancaster), Lancaster City Archives, Lancaster, LA1 4AW

Ross Men's Hockey Club, Hereford Records Office, Hereford HR1 2QX

Royal Portsmouth Yacht Club, Portsmouth Records Office, PO1 2LE

Northern Rugby League Football Union, Minutes, Rugby League Headquarters, Leeds, LS2 4SJ

Rugeley Bowling Green, Staffordshire Record Office, ST16 2LZ (Dobson Collection)

Society of Staffordshire Bowmen, Staffordshire Records, ST16 2LZ (Farley Hill Papers)

South Durham Steeple Chase, Durham County Records, DH1 5UL (D/X/48011)

Southampton Court Leet Records, Southampton City Archive (1569, M41)

South Saxon Archers, East Sussex Records, Lewes, BN7 1UN (SHR 3703-5)

Stafford Races, William Salt Library, Stafford, ST16 2LZ

Stansted Park Cricket Club, Essex Records, Chelmsford, CM1 1LX (T/P68/55/6)

Stayley Hunt, Manchester City Archives, M2 5PD (DD 96/2)

Stockport Races, Stockport Central Library, SK1 3RS

Sunningdale Ladies Golf Club, Berkshire Records, Reading, RG2 9XD (DIEX 53112)

Sutton Sports, Cambridgeshire Records, CB2 0AP (R79/95)

Tees Salmon Fisheries, Durham Records, DH1 5UL (D/St/Box 144)

Thames Rowing Club, Club notice in Minutes, April 1861

Tottenham Hotspur FC, Haringey Museum, Arts Dept., N17 SNU

Tring Village Football Association, Hertfordshire Records, SG1 SDE (AR 138/79. DIX 675)

Trowbridge Recreation Club, Wiltshire Records, Trowbridge, BA14 8JG (WRO.583)

Tyldesley Cricket Club, Wigan Record Office, Leigh, WN7 2DY (D/DS 16)

Tyldesley Swimming Club, Wigan Record Office, Leigh, WN7 2DY (D/DS 16)

Vale of Derwentwater Angling Association, Cumbria Records, Carlisle, CA3 8UR (DISO/67)

Walsall Cricket Club, William Salt Library, Stafford, ST16 2LZ

Walsall Cycling and Running Club, Walsall Central Archives, WS1 1TR (3103)

Walthamstow Bicycle Club, Waltham Forest Library, E17 9NH (W37.3875. WBC.2)

Walthamstow Ferry Fishery Society, Waltham Forest Library, E17 9NH

Warrington Anglers Association, Central Library, Warrington, WA1 1JB

Walthamstow Tennis and Bowling Club, Waltham Forest Library, E17 9NH

Warrington Golf Club, Central Library, Warrington, WA1 1JB

Warrington Parks Bowling League, Central Library, Warrington WA1 1JB

Warrington Sailing Club, Central Library, Warrington, WA1 1JB

Warrington Swimming Club, Central Library, Warrington, WA1 1JB

Warwick Angling Society, Warwick County Records, CV34 4JS (W37.223.WI)

Warwick Races 1754, Warwick County Records, CV34 4JS (CR229/Box 2/2)

Westbourne Recreation Club, East Sussex Records, BN7 1UN

West Kent Wanderers Cricket Club, Lewisham Archives, SE13 5SY

Whitfield Cricket Club, Northumberland Record Office, NE3 5QX

Wood Green Cricket Club, Haringey Museum, N17 8NU

Worcester Tricycle Club, City of Worcester Record Office, Worcester, WR1 1TN

Worksop Cricket Club, Nottinghamshire Records, NG1 1HR (DD4P 62110814)

Other original sources

Accounts of a Dancing Master, Nottinghamshire Records, NG 1 1HR (DD 5P.7)

Bearbaiting in Cambridge, Cambridgeshire Records, CB2 0AP (PB vol. 31)

Charles Shaw's Shooting Diary, Northamptonshire Records, NN4 9AW

Death of Lord Shaftsbury's Son, Northumberland Record Office, NE3 5QX (ZMI/576.50)

Edward Harbottle Grimston's Diary, Hertfordshire Records, SG1 8DE (DIEV/F154)

Game Duty Certificates 1802, 1824, Buckinghamshire Museum, Aylesbury, HP20 2QP

Horse Racing on Skircoate Moor, Calderdale Archives, Halifax, HX1 5LA (Misc. 3–4)

Mass Observation Archive, Survey of Worcester, October 1940

Mass Observation Archive, April 1942 (weekly intelligence service) University of Sussex

Sport England, *Investing for Our Sporting Future: 1999–2009* (Sport England, 1999)

Prize Fighting in Cambridge, Cambridgeshire Records, CB2 0AP

INDEX

191